Minority Teacher Recruitment and Retention Strategies

Janet E. Kearney-Gissendaner, Ph.D.

EYE ON EDUCATION

Eye on Education
6 Depot Way West, Suite 106
Larchmont, NY 10538
(914) 833-0551
(914) 833-0761 fax
www.eyeoneducation.com

For information about permission to reproduce selections
from this book, write: Eye On Education, Permissions Dept.,
Suite 106, 6 Depot Way West, Larchmont, NY 10538

Library of Congress Cataloging-in-Publication Data

Kearney, Janet E.
Minority teacher recruitment and retention strategies/
by Janet E. Kearney.
        p.   cm.
Includes bibliographical references.
ISBN 978-1-59667-152-2
1. Minority teachers—Recruiting—United States.
2. Minority teachers—Training of—United States.
3. Minority teachers—Employment—United States.
4. Teacher turnover—United States. I. Title.

LB2835.25.K43 2010
331.12'313711—dc22   2010004801

10 9 8 7 6 5 4 3

Also Available from EYE ON EDUCATION

Leading School Change:
Strategies to Bring Everybody On Board
Todd Whitaker

Get Organized!
Time Management for School Leaders
Frank Buck

Executive Skills for Busy School Leaders
Chris Hitch and David Coley

Classroom Walkthroughs to Improve Teaching and Learning
Kachur, Stout and Edwards

Rigorous Schools and Classrooms:
Leading the Way
Ronald Williamson and Barbara R. Blackburn

Professional Learning Communities:
An Implementation Guide and Toolkit
Kathleen A. Foord and Jean M. Haar

Professional Development: What Works
Sally J. Zepeda

152 Ways to Keep Students in School:
Franklin P. Schargel

Creating School Cultures that Embrace Learning:
What Successful Leaders Do
Tony Thacker, John S. Bell and Franklin P. Schargel

From At-Risk to Academic Excellence:
What Successful Leaders Do
Franklin P. Schargel, Tony Thacker and John S. Bell

Meet the Author

Dr. Janet Kearney-Gissendaner is an Associate Professor of Education Administration at Ashland University in Ohio. A former school administrator and teacher, she had managed personnel administration services for a large urban district and had served as a middle and high school teacher and assistant principal. She has also held special assignment positions in evaluation and research services and pupil/community relations.

Dr. Kearney-Gissendaner has received numerous awards, recognitions and citations, most recently the Ashland University Mentor Award. Honorary membership awards were presented to Dr. Kearney-Gissendaner from the Ohio and national associations of school personnel administrators for her contributions to the field. The Bill Hunter Award was presented to her for outstanding work in personnel administration in the state of Ohio. She is a former president of the Ohio Association of School Personnel Administrators where she remains active as a liaison on the board for the Ohio minority teacher recruitment consortium (OMRC). She presently chairs the Council Attracting Prospective Educators (CAPE) for the state of Ohio, which promotes a development of a pipeline of future teachers for Ohio schools.

Dr. Kearney-Gissendaner's publications, presentations, and workshops focus on providing school districts and organizations with information to build and sustain programs for addressing the issues of shortages focused on minority teachers and other teachers needed in our classrooms. Her scholarly work has appeared in the Best Practices of the American Association of School Personnel Administrators publications, The Ohio ASCD Journal, Education and Urban Society Journal, and the Mid-Western Educational Research Association (MWERA). She is a member of the Ohio Council of Professors of Educational Association (OCPEA) and remains active in numerous associations related to her research and teaching.

Table of Contents

Preface

The challenge of providing quality minority teachers each decade continues to be the number one issue for all school districts across this nation. It is time to implement program plans for minority teacher recruitment and retention that will work in your school or district and produce results over time! It is not a quick and easy process. Based on my many years of study and research on the topic of minority teacher recruitment and retention, this book will provide information and resources for the purpose of building successful minority teacher recruitment programs that may be implemented seamlessly into your program of work. Chapter 1 emphasizes the statistics surrounding the teacher shortages, the causes, and the need for change. Theoretical underpinnings summarize recent research on the importance of having teachers of color for both white and minority students. Chapter 2 provides information on how this research began and the importance of the urgency to take action on finding minority teachers for school districts across the nation. Chapter 3 contains exemplary minority teacher recruitment model descriptions that can be implemented in districts to meet current needs. Chapter 4 documents pipeline programs, including Grow Your Own models, that help identify students who are interested in the field of teaching education and that target adults and alternative strategies in recruitment of quality teachers with emphasis on minority/diverse populations. An action plan is included in Chapter 5 as well as a listing of all stakeholders (human resource officials, superintendents, principals, teachers, and all who collaborate and connect with the teaching force, including the community to detail action for needed change).

The importance of stakeholder responsibilities is included to emphasize their roles in ensuring that all constituencies are working harmoniously in reaching the ultimate goal of providing a cadre of minority teachers to meet district needs on an annual basis. The action plan includes steps to follow in setting up your minority teacher recruitment program.

There is no easy path to achieving success in building a minority teacher recruitment model that will produce immediate results for a school district or organization. As all stakeholders work on component parts to make the circle complete, the positive results of their efforts will be quality teachers serving the nation's students. This information is provided as an impetus for districts to create a model to meet students' needs, enhance one already in operation, and share successes, failures, and future endeavors to make a profound difference for our nation's students.

How will this book helps district personnel officials, superintendents, principals, building and central office administrators, and all stakeholders of education? It will:

♦ Provide pertinent information on the minority teacher shortage and the need for immediate short-term and long-term action goals.
♦ Provide minority recruitment program development with detailed conceptual outlines, program depth or strategies, tools to use, steps to emulate programs, information for model development, a listing of programs nationwide, and steps to sell the idea or program to the district.
♦ Show how to work with your stakeholders in planting seeds of growth, support (including financial backing for programs), assertiveness in connecting, and collaborating with the human resource function to produce continuous results of finding and keeping minority teachers for all children. Below is a chart depicting the stakeholders important to the process. You may want to add additional persons as you begin to think about your respective district and situation.

Acknowledgements

I am grateful to many people who stimulated my thinking and contributed to this book. My sincere appreciation is extended to the American Association of School Personnel Administrators Association (AASPA), who supported the idea and provided valuable information and resources. I am indebted to personnel administrators and colleagues across the nation who contributed their ideas and models included in this book.

Special thanks to Carla Edlefson, Professor, Ashland University, who spent much time reading my work and providing valuable feedback. And to Mary Crabtree, Administrative Assistant, Columbus Ohio City School District who was always there to type and attend to the presentation of my work in record time!

I thank the reviewers who conscientiously read the manuscript and spent valuable time providing me with their insightful information.

I wish to acknowledge my dear husband, Fred Gissendaner, who is always there to provide a creative perspective, a listening ear, and who spurs me on to the finish line!

Finally, I will always be indebted to my mother and father who instilled in me a passion for learning and a focus for achievement.

1

A Critical Examination of Teacher Shortages: Thoughts on Needed Change

A Compelling Unsolved Challenge

Public school districts across the nation are alarmed by the continued severe shortages of teachers, African-American, and other races. Minority teacher shortages have continued to worsen for over four decades, and school district officials need programs that work to sustain recruitment, selection, and retention of quality minority teachers. This compelling problem is of national significance because classrooms are multicultural in nature (Recruiting New Teachers, 1994). There is an urgent need for teachers who represent many cultures to teach our students. This need did not come about recently, but dates back to school systems in the throes of implementing desegregation after the *Brown v. Education* decision. At that time, 80% of the school population was white and 20% was minority. By 1996, the number of minority students had risen to approximately 35% of the student population; and today it stands at nearly 40% and growing (Torres, Santos, Peck, & Cortes, 2004). It is no wonder that minority teacher shortages have been a hot topic spanning four decades. While percentages of minority students are high and growing, a daunting task is before us to increase the number of minority teachers available for this growing population of minority students as well as to provide role models for nonminority students.

Student diversity remains in stark contrast to teacher diversity. According to Torres et al., the American Association of Colleges for Teacher Education (AACTE; 2004), in 1997 reported that the vast majority of teachers in our schools and in teacher preparation programs were white (87%) and female (74%). In 1977, minority teachers constituted approximately 12.2% of the total number of teachers. More recent estimates indicate that the percentage of white teachers in public schools is as high as 90%, meaning that the percentage of minority teachers may have decreased to 9% (Torres et al., 2004, p. 3). The recent advent of the baby boomer retirement has made an enormous impact on America's elementary and secondary school classrooms leaving a void in the number of available teachers who had years of accumulated knowledge and experience—a void which will only worsen in the coming decade. This is compounded by what is happening at the other end of the pipeline. As young teachers are dropping out, the number of minority students, especially Hispanics, is steeply rising; but the teaching pool remains almost exclusively white (Duarte, 2000, pp. 19–23).

According to a report of the Northwest Regional Laboratory (NWREL), 1997, when teachers of color are missing, minority students land in more special education classes, have higher absentee rates, and tend to be less involved in activities (p. 1).

According to the NWREL report, the Education Trust, a Washington, DC–based nonprofit organization that works to reduce the achievement gap, notes that "data from schools show that lower income children and children of color can excel if they are taught at high levels" (p. 1). Research shows many other factors influence this achievement gap. Some important ones are family involvement, cultural differences, expectations, grouping arrangements, and English language acquisition (p. 1).

The Office of Educational Research and Improvement (OERI), U.S. Department of Education, sponsored, in part, the following information regarding elements that enhance the achievement, attitudes, and behavior of minority group students. These have been summarized in part by NWREL (2001, p. 13).

1. Strong leadership on the part of school administrators
2. Teachers who believe they are responsible for students' learning and capable of teaching them effectively
3. High expectations for student learning and behavior on the part of administrators and teachers
4. Safe and orderly, well-disciplined, but not rigid school environment

5. Teachers who are adept at modifying instructional materials and strategies in response to students' differing learning styles and needs
6. Recruitment and hiring of minority teachers

Causes of Teacher Shortages

Knowing some of the causes of teacher shortages, particularly those pointed out by Haberman (2005), turns us in a direction of recruitment and retention that must be built and sustained over time. Nourishing the pipeline of prospective teachers will be a critical factor in providing a solid baseline of qualified teachers in all licensure areas for the future.

Haberman describes the length of an average teaching career being eleven years. Teachers who decide to pursue lifelong careers in the classrooms are now clearly the exception (p. 3). He further states that the majority of those who graduate from traditional education programs never take jobs as teachers.

> In 2001, sixty-one percent of the newly certified graduates did not take teaching jobs. This lower figure does not mean more teachers entered classrooms, however, since the total number produced in 2001 had declined by almost 20 percent. These nonteaching certified graduates frequently referred to by many as 'fully qualified' don't take teaching positions because the jobs are primarily in urban schools serving diverse children in poverty. (Haberman, p. 31)

Haberman (2005) also mentions this reason as yet another cause for the teacher shortage. He further emphasized that the young white adults who compose over 90% of the traditionally trained teachers simply "don't want or cannot relate to diverse children and youth in urban poverty" (p. 4).

A third reason for the teacher shortage Haberman notes is the number of beginners who take jobs in urban schools but fail or leave. Based on data from the National Center for Educational

Statistics School and Staffing Survey, school staffing problems were seen to be primarily due to excess demand resulting from a revolving door where large numbers of teachers depart for reasons other than retirement (p. 4). Haberman (2005) reported that, in his own city, half of the new teachers were gone in three years or less and that many quit in the first year.

A fourth reason Haberman (2005) posed for the teacher shortage in urban schools is the shortage of special education teachers. Haberman states, "This shortage is exacerbated by the practice of many suburbs, small towns, parochial and private schools contracting out the education of their children with special needs to nearby urban school districts." He contends that it not only increases the shortage in urban districts, but raises costs (p. 4). And, typically, these shortages projected by Haberman in special education and math are experienced by many districts across the nation. Additionally, districts across our nation randomly report that shortages occur in some foreign languages, dual certification and licensed teachers, and some areas of science.

Other reasons for teacher shortages that Haberman (2005) projects are:

- the greater entrance level career opportunities now available to women outside of teaching
- college graduates of color who now have greater access to larger numbers of careers than in former times
- math and science teachers leaving at a higher rate than others, many of whom are men seeking better opportunities

Need for Change

The American Association for School Personnel Administrators (AASPA) recognized the need for a publication to provide their membership with information on successful minority teacher recruitment models nationwide to address the challenges of minority teacher shortages. AASPA provided data on minority teacher percentages from member districts and provided a forum for the author to work with data provided by member school districts on numbers and percentages of minority teachers in districts represented during a two-year period. The author chaired an ad hoc minority recruitment committee of AASPA for the purpose of finding successful minority recruitment models nationwide and then directed action plans to showcase respective district model plans that work to produce and retain quality minority teachers. These model plans, representing urban, suburban, rural, and combinations of plans, provide excellent ideas for districts or organizations to develop a minority recruitment model suited for their school district or organization.

Policy development within each district or organization solidifies commitment to this process; Grow Your Own programs will plant the seed which needs constant nurturing. Minority teacher recruitment on historically black college campuses will provide visualization for students, enabling these prospective teachers on campuses across the nation to realize the compelling need to commit to the teaching profession!

The benefits of having minority teachers in the classroom include positive role models for minority and majority students alike, increased cultural sensitivity, bridging the achievement gap and exits for many minority students, and frequent bilingual abilities. Citing these benefits, scholars are alarmed by the fact that minority teacher representation today in our public schools is only around 3% of the total pool of teachers. It is no wonder that minority teacher shortages have emerged over the past five decades as among the most burning educational issues.

Demands on Minority Teacher Hiring

Knowing that American's school age population has become more multicultural and multiethnic, and its teaching workforce reflects a trend in the opposite direction, it is logical that teachers of color are in high demand in all subjects, grade levels, and geographic areas as reported by Recruiting New Teachers, 2004. In Recruiting New Teachers' 2000 study of the largest urban school districts, almost 73% of the responding districts reported an immediate need for teachers of color. The 2003 National Commission on Teaching and America's Future reported that individuals of African-American, Hispanic and Latino, Asian, and Native American descent make up 14% of K–12 teachers, while 36% of students are from such backgrounds (Recruiting New Teachers, 2004).

Minority Teacher Deficit: Lessons Learned

Torres et al., 2004, summarize and argue the review of literature in the field of minority teacher recruitment, development, and retention. Recent research is discussed regarding the contributions of teachers of color to the education of both white and minority students. There are primary lessons to be learned from this information to ready ourselves in taking on this monumental challenge we face in combating the current minority teacher shortage today!

The first lesson is the history of the present minority teacher shortage. Historically, the teaching profession was extremely important to the African-American people. Prior to the Civil Rights Act of 1964, it was reported that most college-educated African Americans were in the teaching profession. And, in 1954, approximately 82,000 African-American teachers were responsible for the education of 2 million African-American public school students. But by 1964, at least 38,000 of the 82,000 African-American educators nationwide had lost their teaching positions (Torres et al., 2004).

The underrepresentation of the minority teachers seems to have been an unintended side effect of the partial implementation of desegregation following the Supreme Court decision in *Brown v. Board of Education* (1954). While minority students were transferred in some numbers into majority-white schools, African-American teachers were transferred with far less frequency. There were no provisions made at that time to integrate school faculties, administrations, and staff. Instead, African-American teachers and administrators were either dismissed or demoted, and the schools hired white teachers and administrators to deal with the increase in student population, according to Torres et al., 2004.

This set the stage for the following struggle surrounding the condition of the minority teacher in the United States as the the lack of commitment to having a diverse teaching staff ultimately affected the pipeline for minority teachers to enter the profession.

Many issues worked greatly to limit the number of African-American teachers in the profession following the *Brown v. Board of Education* decision: for example, teacher testing, certification, and salary differentials. The testing requirements began in the South and did not become law in other states until the mid-1980s. Personnel and human resource officials in states without testing recruited southern minority teachers whose coursework met certification requirements in their states. They offered higher salaries without having to require testing as in the South. This incentive was used to lure prospective teachers from the South to the North and continued well in to the early 1990s until state boards of education changed the requirements for certification and instituted the National Teacher Exam (NTE) in additional states. Time frames were set for teachers to meet requirements, and those teachers who were unable to comply were terminated. These were short-lived strategies since testing and the recent advent of the No Child Left Behind Act posed additional challenges for minority prospective teachers as well as teachers already in the profession working to meet additional certification and licensure requirements.

Today: The Impetus for Change

We need now, more than ever, to implement programs that influence minority students to enter teaching and help them through the pipeline, provide opportunities for employment, and retain them for leading our children across the nation. We also need to retain the "bright shining stars" (teachers) whom we already have in the teaching force.

Therefore, to avoid losing ground on providing a minority teaching force of excellence, we must do the following:

a) constantly review the existing research on the impact of teachers of color; b) expand our research base on culturally responsive teaching and the role that ethnicity plays in fostering student achievement; c) study the pipeline to teaching to identify a variety of institutional conditions and practices that limit access, prompt failure, and create hostile learning environments for prospective teachers of color; d) redesign teacher preparation and curricula to effectively address issues of diversity and culturally responsive teaching; e) develop high quality alternative teacher preparation models; f) address teacher assessment issues, in particular the impact of teacher competency testing on the pool of prospective teachers of color; g) study the role that standardized assessment has in K–12 education; h) provide greater resources for carrying out missions of new accountability measures; and i) address the need for greater resources targeted to the recruitment, preparation, and support of a teaching cadre (National Summit on Diversity in the Teaching Force, 2002, pp. 7–9).

To accomplish the above initiatives, we must prepare to take immediate action in our own districts and to collaborate with fellow school districts, colleges and universities, the community, and businesses alike.

Torres et al., 2004, insist that, if more minorities were successfully completing high school and college, the problem of underrepresentation would be of less concern. The Grow Your Own programs implemented across the United States have emphasized the importance of finding new approaches to solving this critical teacher shortage. These programs are operating in elementary, middle, and high schools introducing students to the "world of teaching." Teacher advisors develop and implement a program whereby students meet and participate in hands-on activities at their respective schools and in their communities to learn about the field of education.

The Future Educators of America also operates through Phi Delta Kappa to provide middle and high school students with opportunities to explore teaching as a career option. The Council for Attracting Prospective Educators (CAPE) is yet another strategy for "growing teachers" operating in the state of Ohio. This strategy was modeled after a Phi Delta Kappa program targeting prospective teachers of color. Board leadership for this program represents a cross section of interested people including personnel officials, college or university educators, administrators, U.S. Department of Education officials, and board of regents' representatives. The goal of the program is to assess the impact of career choice and knowledge about education careers (Kearney, 2004).

It is important for human resource officials to remember that attrition in the potential pool of minority teachers begins in high schools, according to Torres et al., 2004, and that minority teacher shortages cannot be attributed solely to fewer minorities choosing to enter the teaching profession. The teacher pipeline is a determining factor in this process. This clearly points to the importance of building programs to "grow teachers" and connect with the universities to support them throughout their college careers. Then, we must use tracking methods to select and hire the best and brightest teachers for our nation's students.

To meet the wave of high standards of the future, the importance of preparing a potential teacher pool of the future becomes even more critical. Rigorous preparation must begin in grades K–12. Some suggestions for strategies include targeting minority students as early as middle school. School districts, armed with this information, must consider further steps at the high school level to develop teacher academies. Such programs have been developed across the country to provide opportunities of study in education to high school students. These programs stimulate and foster interest in the teaching profession while providing a rigorous but basic academic program with an emphasis on college preparation. Students who successfully complete these academy programs (which operate within a high school of the district) could access eligibility for tuition scholarships to the university that agreed to be a partner of the program. Support may be represented by multiple colleges and universities. There is no doubt that such partnerships and collaborative strategies strengthen the minority pipeline. Program articulation and collaboration between two- and four-year colleges help fund recruitment efforts and instructional programs.

It is also helpful to the entire program to coordinate programs such as Future Educators to continue to "grow" teachers from all levels of the student ranks. These programs led by chosen teacher advisors will provide a pool of available students for the academy and other interested students who will pursue education when entering college. This comprehensive approach utilizing sources of students within the local system and partnering with colleges and universities will build community in one's "own backyard."

Testing is an important part of helping students along the pipeline to teaching. There is reliable evidence that competency testing poses obstacles to minority teacher candidates. Nearly all states have created policies that require potential teachers to take as many as six tests throughout the pipeline, beginning in some states with the high school graduation tests. Early intervention and continuous preparation for the exam is very important for African-American and Hispanic students. In addition, college faculty must infuse critical thinking throughout the curriculum and use professional educational terms aligned with the competencies to be tested. School districts may form partnerships with the university to team teach with talented and qualified staff in targeted content areas, thereby providing a strong link of theory and practice. Consideration of alternative assessments that include individual portfolios of preservice experiences in the classroom as an additional or alternative way of measuring teaching quality would be helpful to prospective teachers.

Recruitment of minority teachers also includes those who possess much experience. Suggestions include the following actions to increase the recruitment and retention of this group: a) provide continuing professional development; b) encourage collaborative relationships with schools; and c) provide financial and other incentives, although there is little or no research on the effectiveness of financial incentives.

In order to channel teachers to hard-to-staff and low-performing schools, financial incentives must be offered. Districts may offer a 20% increase over other comparable salaries and create financing for teachers that could be offered in the following ways:

◆ Housing assistance, particularly in urban areas where housing costs are prohibitive for a teacher on beginning salary scales

- ◆ Signing bonuses for new teachers hired to teach in challenging school environments and/or critical-demand subject areas
- ◆ Salary increases. Salaries vary from region to region and state to state.

Personnel and human resource officials should work with state departments of education in each state across the nation to create a more flexible system in allowing teachers to remain certified when moving from one state to another. The licensure and certification process is cumbersome and inhibits flexibility in recruiting teachers from other states.

Other strategies to recruit minority teachers may include: a) developing a strong marketing and outreach campaign by advertising in minority publications such as *The Black Collegian;* b) developing community partnerships to support recruitment and retention of minority candidates (for example, contacts that help link schools with minority networks such as church groups, fraternities and sororities on campuses, and alumni in the communities; c) seeking out minority interns from neighboring teacher education programs and sending a multiethnic team to attend career days at predominantly minority colleges; d) assisting teachers of color by creating a support system; and e) recruiting minority candidates who transfer from other professions or retirees and other teachers and community members to help new teachers.

Preparing minority student prospective teachers and sustaining them to the finish line of teacher education and preparation is so essential!

Discussion

My review of the literature had a major impact on me as far as how one should feel about the recruitment, selection, retention, and building program and strategies for sustained growth in providing quality minority teachers for our nation's children. Knowing the historical underpinnings of the shortages and the body of research that relate to this issue places in perspective one's understanding of the whole notion of the minority teacher recruitment and retention and development of programs. Therefore, it is my belief that to address these issues no one method or strategy will work exclusively, but data must continue to drive decisions; policies must be enacted to provide a foundation for direction; collaborative work must ensue to nourish the pipeline of teachers; and partnerships must be actively pursued with universities, school districts, and businesses to build cutting edge programs.

Marketing and highlighting the programs that are offered in districts, for example, Grow Your Own and others, will give prospective teachers positive feedback about entering the profession. Helping them escape barriers to certification, negative perceptions of the profession, inequities in testing, college admission, and incongruence of their experiences with traditional teacher education curricula will make a difference in developing quality teachers and retaining them.

A system for evaluating program models must be developed and used. For example, many alternative programs that were developed in schools and institutions began as Grow Your Own programs. They were used to find teacher candidates for teacher preparation. Over the years, the quality of these programs was questioned. Evidence was needed to confirm what specific program components and characteristics were most important in preparing minorities for careers in teaching.

According to Torres et al., 2004, roughly 25% of beginning teachers do not return for their third year; estimates of five-year attrition rates vary but suggest that about half of all new teachers leave the profession in their first five years.

Attention needs to be paid to retention of teachers. Ongoing analysis is needed for patterns of minority teacher retention and mobility from one school to another, as well as studies of on-the job experiences that discourage minority teacher retention along with factors that contribute to teacher retention.

An examination of teachers hired over time to determine their satisfaction with various aspects of teaching should occur. Information gleaned from this process would be helpful for policy implementation and commitment to work on areas of support for teachers throughout their careers (Kearney, 1997).

We need to consider policies that increase the diversity of the teacher pool. We also need to prepare all teachers to reach children whose backgrounds are different from their own, and it is recommended that future research ought to be centered on the preparation of teachers to teach diverse students.

More districts nationwide need to publicly commit to a policy of nondiscriminatory hiring and translate this policy into a resolution to be forwarded to their respective legal, legislative, and policy panels of their districts. This will ensure that policy is addressed on increasing the number and percentage of culturally diverse staff members.

We must examine the minority recruitment models in regard to the kinds of support systems that are built into the program development for minority recruitment and retention of teachers. This component is necessary for long-term sustainability of excellent programs.

Consideration must be given to the preparation of teachers who have abilities to reach children whose backgrounds are different from their own. For example, teacher selection must be emphasized, according to Haberman,

> where getting better teachers to do the specific things 'stars' do will: a) produce more children of color who learn more and who can compete for places in high quality schools and universities, and b) open up teaching to more minority teachers who at present are seriously under-represented in the teaching force. (introduction)

The Haberman interview and selection process identifies teachers possessing these characteristics to ensure hiring teachers who can reach children of all backgrounds.

The importance of effective teacher induction must be emphasized to help teacher retention. Unlike doctors and lawyers, novice teachers are placed in full-time positions with little or no help. They are also given challenging assignments. Heavy course loads, limited time for preparation, little active supervision, and generally a lack of professional support are reasons for teacher attrition.

We must think in new terms as Williams (2005) noted:

Educational institutions are being called upon to operate in increasingly complex environments characterized by emerging educational reform policies, increased accountability for fiscal, academic, and social outcomes, challenges relative to identifying and retaining talent, and increasing professional and employment standards. (p. 1)

The time has come to not only dream about resources we need to make a difference in our work, but also to think about the resources we have and use them differently. For example, to have minority teachers who possess license or certification in critical-needs areas provide instruction in a multitude of places, we need to use more technology. As we build our model programs for recruitment and retention of quality minority teachers, we need to think about the scope, rapidity, and complexity of today's discontinuous changes and challenges in educational institutions; more so, individual contributors working within them need to continually reinvent themselves in order to achieve organizational goals, enable professional effectiveness, and compete in the global marketplace (Williams, 2005).

The recruitment models provided in this book offer a dimension to incorporate ideas for the recruitment and retention of minority teachers; to identify a program that could be tailored to your needs; and to grow your own teacher model to recruit and retain teachers for your district. Other programs and resources are included to build pipeline programs and to forge partnerships with schools and universities locally and nationally. Last, it is important to know how stakeholders are vital to this process. What are their responsibilities? This information is important to know as you begin the journey of building a successful minority recruitment program to meet your district's need.

2

Identification of Recruitment Models Focused on Minority Teachers: A Theoretical Concept and Survey

The Challenge for Practitioners to Devise Successful Minority Teacher Programs

For each model district described in this book, researchers uncovered information congruent with the "recruitment theory concept" (Davis, 1994; Noeth, Engen, & Noeth, 1984; Ribak-Rosenthal, 1994). This theory describes factors that affect career decisions and that are found to be relatively consistent across all professional fields of study. It is important to note that people who influence career decisions include family members, friends, peers, teachers, counselors, and other role models (Winston, 1997). Other factors that affect career decisions are the quality of the coursework, ability to obtain good grades in the coursework, extra curricular activities augmenting the field of study, and work experience (internships).

Practitioners in the field who ponder this theory and the key factors that influence career decisions will find the impetus to devise long-lasting program strategies for finding adequate numbers of minority teachers for our nation's students.

Losing Ground: A National Summit on Diversity in the Teaching Force, held on February 15, 2002, was germane to our focus as to how we as a nation are "losing ground" on ensuring a teaching force of excellence and diversity for the nation's schools (National Summit on Diversity in the Teaching Force, 2002). Participants represented the American Association of Colleges for Teacher Education, American Council on Education, Association of Teacher Educators, Community Teachers Institute, National Education Association, Recruiting New Teachers, Inc., and the American Association of School

Personnel Administrators (AASPA). These energetic and concerned participants expressed a commitment to make a measurable difference to ensure a teaching force of excellence and diversity for our nation's students. Throughout three days of conference presentations and discussion, summit participants focused on the relationships among educational opportunity, educational achievement, educator diversity, and teacher quality. In particular, the roles of ethnicity and cultural competence were assessed with respect to their impact on student achievement. It was determined that there was a need to disseminate existing research on the impact of teachers of color and a need to expand the research base on culturally responsive teaching and the role that ethnicity plays in fostering student achievement.
Further,

> Data were presented on the growing diversity of the nation's school age population and the demographic composition of its teaching force, which has remained virtually static for teachers of color over the past decades. There was widespread concern among the participants about the implications of these demographic disparities and overwhelming consensus that this lack of teaching force diversity has a negative impact on the quality of education for all children, since children need role models to represent all races. Policies and practices that either promote or inhibit the participation of underrepresented groups were identified, and participants called for action in seven general areas: a) research, b) pipeline issues, c) institutional and program practices, d) teacher preparation and curricula, e) teacher assessment, f) accountability, and g) institutional resources. (National Summit on Diversity in the Teaching Force. pp. 7–12)

The author worked with the AASPA membership to identify successful minority teacher recruitment models nationwide that address the challenges of minority teacher shortages. These successful models and minority recruitment survey data will provide ideas for recruiting and retaining minority teachers in districts across the nation. Additionally, ideas, tools, and strategies will be provided for all stakeholders of education in the development of a minority teacher recruitment model that will serve respective districts and organizations. It is the author's hope that these models will be helpful to readers who desire to continue to build innovative programs. Further, we encourage other districts to contribute their own exemplary models for future editions of this publication.

The AASPA Survey Information on Minority Teacher Programs

The American Association for School Personnel Administrators (AASPA) survey to members resulted in obtaining valuable information on numbers and percentages of teachers hired in districts during the hiring 2004–2005 (Table 2.1) and 2005–2006 (Table 2.2) school years. The exemplary models are included with these data and show good working numbers and percentages of minority teacher hires.

The data from the thirty-three school districts responding to the survey reflect patterns of minority hiring similar to those reported in the review literature, which indicates available minority teacher percentages as low as 9% for diverse teachers. Only a couple of suburban districts fell below that figure. Higher percentages of minority hires almost always occurred in urban districts with the exception of a few rural districts in the southern states where up to 25% of teachers hired were minority. The 2005–2006 school year yielded slightly higher percentages in the urban districts and southern rural districts. More districts reported hiring over 25% minority teachers in 2005–2006 than did in 2004–2005. Reported numbers of total hires for both years indicated most minority teachers were hired in urban and suburban areas. This was off-set with higher numbers in a few rural areas in the Deep South.

TABLE 2.1 School District Hiring Data (AASPA), School Years 2004-05
District Type, Numbers, Percentages, and Race of Teacher Hires

School District	District Type	Total Hires	% Caucasian	% Black	% Hispanic	% Alaskan/ Native American	% Asian
ACES	Suburban/Urban	10	100.0%	0.0%	0.0%	0.0%	0.0%
Albermarle	Suburban/Rural	152	88.2%	5.9%	3.9%	0.0%	2.0%
Ames	Rural	32	91.0%	6.0%	3.0%	0.0%	0.0%
Anne Arundel	Suburban	831	85.0%	11.0%	2.0%	1.0%	1.0%
Asheville	Urban	46	81.0%	13.0%	4.0%	2.0%	0.0%
Bellevue	Suburban	70	93.0%	3.0%	4.0%	0.0%	0.0%
Bilohio	Urban	40	70.0%	20.0%	10.0%	0.0%	0.0%
Birdville	Suburban	285	91.0%	4.0%	5.0%	0.0%	0.0%
Camera	Suburban/Urban	464.5	79.5%	19.4%	0.9%	0.0%	0.2

TABLE 2.1 School District Hiring Data (AASPA), School Years 2004-05 District Type, Numbers, Percentages, and Race of Teacher Hires *(continued)*

School District	District Type	Total Hires	% Caucasian	% Black	% Hispanic	% Alaskan/ Native American	% Asian
Carrollton-Farmers	Suburban	295	81.0%	5.4%	12.2%	0.7%	0.7%
Charleston	Suburban/Urban Rural	470	86.0%	12.0%	3.0%	0.0%	1.0%
Charlottesville	Urban	60	88.0%	12.0%	0.0%	0.0%	0.0%
Chesterfield	Suburban	460	86.0%	11.0%	1.0%	1.0%	1.0%
Des Moines	Urban	575	74.9%	17.9%	5.1%	0.0%	2.1%
Dothan	Rural	120	74.0%	25.0%	1.0%	0.0%	0.0%
Dublin	Surburban	83	91.0%	6.0%	3.0%	0.0%	0.0%
East Greenbush	Surburban	20	90.0%	5.0%	0.0%	0.0%	5.0%
Elgin	Suburban/Urban	*	86.0%	2.0%	12.0%	0.0%	0.0%

TABLE 2.1 School District Hiring Data (AASPA), School Years 2004-05
District Type, Numbers, Percentages, and Race of Teacher Hires *(continued)*

School District	District Type	Total Hires	% Caucasian	% Black	% Hispanic	% Alaskan/ Native American	% Asian
FairFax	Suburban	365	60.0%	25.0%	18.0%	0.0%	8.0%
Frederick	Suburban	297	94.0%	4.0%	1.0%	0.0%	1.0%
Garland	Suburban	831	75.0%	11.0%	11.0%	1.0%	2.0%
Greenville	Urban	561	88.0%	11.0%	1.0%	0.0%	0.0%
Harford	Suburban	263	89.7%	9.9%	0.4%	0.0%	0.0%
Henrico	Suburban	550	79.0%	19.0%	2.0%	0.0%	0.0%
Kenosha	Urban	275	89.0%	8.0%	2.0%	0.0%	1.0%
Killeen	Surburban	1238	47.0%	30.0%	19.0%	0.0%	4.0%
Lamar	Rural	36	28.0%	7.0%	0.0%	0.0%	1.0%
Loudown	Suburban	700	94.0%	2.0%	2.0%	1.0%	1.0%

TABLE 2.1 School District Hiring Data (AASPA), School Years 2004-05 District Type, Numbers, Percentages, and Race of Teacher Hires *(continued)*

School District	District Type	Total Hires	% Caucasian	% Black	% Hispanic	% Alaskan/ Native American	% Asian
Lubbock	Suburban	230	82.0%	7.0%	11.0%	0.0%	0.0%
Moore County	Other	170	80.0%	17.0%	1.0%	2.0%	0.0%
No Name	Suburban	1000	79.0%	19.0%	1.0%	0.0%	1.0%
Pinellas	Urban	867	85.0%	9.0%	4.0%	1.0%	1.0%
Rochester	Surburban	55	97.0%	1.0%	1.0%	0.0%	2.0%
St. Mary's County	Suburban	148	93.0%	7.0%	0.0%	0.0%	0.0%
Sumner	Suburban	59	86.0%	3.0%	1.0%	0.0%	1.0%
Township	Suburban	70	85.0%	2.0%	7.0%	0.0%	6.0%
West Windsor	Other	98	59.0%	17.0%	5.0%	1.0%	18.0%

*Elgin School district did not report total hires.

TABLE 2.2 School District Hiring Data (AASPA), School Years 2005-06
District Type, Numbers, Percentages, and Race of Teacher Hires

School District	District Type	Total Hires	% Caucasian	% Black	% Hispanic	% Alaskan/ Native American	% Asian
ACES	Suburban/Urban	29	62.0%	17.0%	3.0%	0.0%	0.0%
Albermarle	Suburban/Rural	162	91.9%	5.6%	0.6%	0.6%	1.2%
Ames	Rural	19	95.0%	5.0%	0.0%	0.0%	0.0%
Anne Arundel	Suburban	792	85.0%	11.0%	2.0%	1.0%	1.0%
Asheville	Urban	52	94.0%	6.0%	0.0%	0.0%	0.0%
Bellevue	Suburban	75	93.0%	5.0%	2.0%	0.0%	0.0%
Bilohio	Urban	23	78.0%	22.0%	0.0%	0.0%	0.0%
Birdville	Suburban	209	87.0%	4.0%	8.0%	0.0%	1.0%
Blue Valley	Suburban	140	97.0%	1.0%	1.0%	1.0%	0.0%
Camera	Suburban/Urban	350	74.9%	23.7%	1.1%	0.0%	0.3%

TABLE 2.2 School District Hiring Data (AASPA), School Years 2005-06 District Type, Numbers, Percentages, and Race of Teacher Hires *(continued)*

School District	District Type	Total Hires	% Caucasian	% Black	% Hispanic	% Alaskan/ Native American	% Asian
Carrollton-Farmers	Suburban	382	73.6%	10.5%	12.0%	0.5%	3.4%
Charleston	Suburban/ UrbanRural	574	83.0%	17.0%	0.0%	0.0%	0.0%
Charlottesville	Urban	85	85.0%	15.0%	0.0%	0.0%	0.0%
Chesterfield	Suburban	554	84.0%	13.0%	2.0%	1.0%	0.0%
Des Moines	Urban	660	83.0%	12.6%	2.9%	15.0%	1.4%
Dothan	Rural	125	70.0%	29.0%	1.0%	0.0%	0.0%
Dublin	Surburban	71	94.0%	3.0%	3.0%	0.0%	0.0%
East Greenbush	Surburban	25	100.0%	0.0%	0.0%	0.0%	0.0%
Elgin	Suburban/Urban	365	70.0%	4.0%	24.0%	0.0%	2.0%
FairFax	Suburban	370	57.0%	30.0%	17.0%	0.0%	6.0%

TABLE 2.2 School District Hiring Data (AASPA), School Years 2005-06 District Type, Numbers, Percentages, and Race of Teacher Hires *(continued)*

School District	District Type	Total Hires	% Caucasian	% Black	% Hispanic	% Alaskan/ Native American	% Asian
Frederick	Suburban	384	94.0%	3.0%	2.0%	0.0%	1.0%
Garland	Suburban	632	65.0%	14.0%	17.0%	1.0%	3.0%
Greenville	Urban	725	89.0%	10.0%	1.0%	0.0%	0.0%
Harford	Suburban	419	92.0%	7.0%	1.0%	0.0%	0.0%
Henrico	Suburban	580	79.0%	20.0%	1.0%	0.0%	0.0%
Kenosha	Urban	200	89.0%	5.0%	5.0%	0.0%	1.0%
Killeen	Surburban	1158	51.0%	28.0%	18.0%	0.0%	3.0%
Lamar	Rural	44	89.0%	9.0%	0.0%	0.0%	2.0%
Loudown	Suburban	750	85.0%	6.0%	4.0%	1.0%	4.0%
Lubbock	Suburban	234	82.9%	4.3%	11.5%	0.0%	1.3%

TABLE 2.2 School District Hiring Data (AASPA), School Years 2005–06 District Type, Numbers, Percentages, and Race of Teacher Hires (*continued*)

School District	District Type	Total Hires	% Caucasian	% Black	% Hispanic	% Alaskan/ Native American	% Asian
Moore County	Other	119	82.0%	16.0%	1.0%	0.0%	1.0%
No Name	Suburban	1000	70.0%	26.0%	2.0%	0.0%	2.0%
Pinellas	Urban	670	84.0%	10.0%	4.0%	1.0%	1.0%
Rochester	Surburban	65	90.0%	3.0%	0.0%	0.0%	2.0%
St. Mary's County	Suburban	160	85.0%	7.0%	5.0%	0.0%	3.0%
Sumner	Suburban	95	97.0%	0.0%	1.0%	0.0%	2.0%
Township	Suburban	85	92.0%	1.0%	4.0%	0.0%	3.0%
West Windsor	Other	88	65.0%	7.0%	10.0%	0.0%	18.0%

AASPA Survey: Paving the Way to Building Collaborative Programs

The AASPA survey asked district officials to provide the following information: a) describe and highlight the diverse recruitment program in your district; b) discuss the features of your program that are successful; c) explain how you evaluate success; d) explain how district or organizational culture affects your program and describe what you do to make people welcome to school, district, and community; e) describe barriers to district efforts to attract and retain minority diverse teachers; f) define an exemplary minority/diverse program; g) describe the strategies you have checked; h) define strategies of minority recruitment program; i) describe outstanding characteristics of minority recruitment model, and your district emphasis; j) explain how you monitor successful programs; and k) discuss recommendations for improvement of minority teacher recruitment program if unlimited resources were provided.

As districts described these categories, definite themes emerged, which are captured in the recruitment strategies survey results on pages 32-33. The recruitment strategies are ranked in order by highest number of responses on given categories. The top strategies identified were in the areas of conducting special recruitment efforts at colleges, recruiting at historically black or Hispanic-serving colleges, providing induction programs and teacher orientation, providing guidance and information about teacher credentialing, sponsoring job fairs to attract new teachers to school districts, offering induction and support programs, establishing partnerships with teacher education programs, offering on the spot contracts, establishing Grow Your Own programs for students in elementary, middle, and high school, and offering teacher academy and professional development activities. The survey information presented provides a wide range of information about minority teacher recruitment and retention initiatives. It is the author's hope that it will be useful for building future programs.

The themes that emerge from these data connect with the research questions and findings of Torres et al., 2004. An example is the "teacher pipeline" issue in which students are making decisions to enter teaching. The Grow Your Own programs and collaborative partnerships with K–12 schools and universities and colleges were mentioned as strategies to nurture that pipeline. Yet another research question posed by Torres et al., 2004, was centered on the recruitment strategies and supports, those most helpful in encouraging and preparing minorities to enter the profession. Those mentioned by survey respondents mirrored the literature: targeting students early on in the process and providing alternate routes to the teaching field. Also, financial incentives were mentioned as an important means of encouragement. Comprehensive recruitment planning inclusive of data collection, evaluating districts' needs, and resources as well as recommendation of changes in policy and practice were mentioned by Torres et al., 2004, as critical components for successful programming. Survey respondents also described their use as means of monitoring their recruitment programs.

It is the hope of the author that this information will be used by human resource and personnel officials to build collaborative programs to further the cause of finding and providing quality minority teachers for our school districts across the nation. It is clear from this information that it is not an easy task, nor is it one that will happen at once. Creativity, ingenuity, resourcefulness, and most of all patience are necessary to succeed in this daunting task! As personnel administrators examine these data, the author challenges all to study the information and decide how recruitment and retention operations may be accomplished differently based on "a new world of work," as coined by Williams (2005) in *Human Resource Executives in the 21st Century Knowledge Age: Partner or Pariah*. Collaboration, partnerships, and nourishing the teacher pipeline are a few of the many avenues to make significant differences in finding quality minority teachers. What other ideas might be brought forward that cause change to occur in hiring minority teachers so that diverse students will be served by a diverse teaching force?

Successful Recruitment Strategies Utilized by Surveyed Districts

Below is a listing of recruitment strategies obtained from the Urban Teacher Challenge (Urban Teacher Collaborative, 2000). School districts (N=33) were surveyed nationwide to gain information on which strategies were used to recruit minority teacher candidates for the nation's schools. The strategies were placed in rank order of high numbers to low numbers of strategies used in respective districts.

No.	Strategies (N=33)
23	Special recruitment efforts at colleges
21	Induction programs and teacher orientation
20	Provide guidance and information about teacher credentialing
19	Sponsor job fairs to attract new teachers to school district
19	Offer induction and support programs
18	Establish partnerships with teacher education programs
17	Recruit at historically black and Hispanic-serving colleges
17	Offer on-the-spot contracts
17	Grow Your Own program for students in elementary, middle, high school
15	Teacher academy, professional development activities
15	Streamline hiring process
15	Offer alternative certification routes
13	Retention strategies for minorities and diversity
11	Utilize alternative licensure procedures, assist out-of-state candidates
9	Incentives (e.g., housing assistance, relocation benefits, financial, salary, etc.)
9	Tuition assistance for graduate course work
9	Participate in online counseling and/or job-finding services or website
8	Offer monetary bonus for talented, high-need subject area candidates

8	International recruitment efforts
7	Non-traditional programs, i.e., Troops to Teachers
7	Incentives for NBPTS certification
6	Provide teacher employment information via telephone hotline
4	Offer bonus for high school achievement
3	Establish searches for nontraditional teachers
2	Offer loan forgiveness program
1	School Placement Guarantees

Minority Teacher Recruitment's Impact on Minority Student Achievement

Key considerations for increasing the teaching ranks of minority teachers are recruitment, development, retention, importance, and impact. As discussed above, Torres et al., 2004, published a thorough literature review in this field. A growing body of research indicates that minority student achievement can be increased when students experience minority teachers in their classrooms (Cotton, 2000; Gurskey, 1990; Johnson & Johnson, 1988). Unfortunately, as minority student populations continued to rise, the percentage of minority teachers dropped dramatically from 1954, when schools were ordered to desegregate under the *Brown v. Board of Education* decision. During the mid-1950s, 80% of the student population in public schools was white; only 20% were minority students. Torres et al., 2004, noted the increase to 40% of the public school population. Researchers have pointed out that a multicultural environment is critical in educating today's youth (Piercynski, Matranga, and Peltier, 1997). These scholars cited the benefits of having minority teachers in the classroom, including providing positive role models for minority and majority students alike, increasing cultural sensitivity, bridging the achievement gap that exists for many minority students, and enhancing bilingual abilities, and they were alarmed that minority teacher representation in our public schools was around only 3% of the total pool of teachers. Minority teacher shortages continue to be among the most burning educational issues.

Five exemplary models presented in this writing detail promising methods and programs in operation that are producing positive results in hiring minority teachers for their respective districts. Their success is measured by teacher candidates who are identified, interviewed, and hired for each school year.

3

Introduction and Information on Five Exemplary Minority Teacher Recruitment Models

Five Exemplary Recruitment Models—Background

The five exemplary models discussed here are Albemarle, the CAMERA (Cleveland Area Minority Education Recruitment Association), Carrollton-Farmers Branch, Des Moines, and Lubbock.

Table 3.1, Racial Composition for the Total Hires, from the AASPA survey, shows that for the exemplary models during school years 2004–2005 and 2005–2006, the highest percentage of teachers hired for all models was in the Caucasian race. (See p. 41). The second highest percentage of teachers hired was in the black race, with exception of the Carrollton-Farmers Branch and the Lubbock school districts located in Texas. These two districts' officials reported Hispanic teachers as the second highest percentage of teacher hires. CAMERA (Cleveland Area Minority Education Recruitment Association) program reported consistently higher percentage rates of teachers of color both years. Des Moines reported higher percentages in the 2004–2005 school year. Carrollton-Farmers, Des Moines, and Albemarle reported higher percentages of Asian/Pacific Islanders than their counterparts.

Overall, each exemplary model reported double digit percentages in hiring teachers of color each year. Even though some percentages were below 20%, there were districts that reported over 20% teachers of color hired in the time frame of 2004–2006. It is important to note that these exemplary models that have such hiring practices are meeting the challenge to recruit teachers of color. Further, these districts participate in special recruitment strategies to build programs and partnerships to nourish the pipeline of minority teachers.

The Urban Teacher Collaborative was founded in 1994 to improve the quality, diversity, and cultural sensitivity of the nation's urban teacher workforce (p. 3). To visualize a picture of teacher supply and preparation challenges in the nation's largest urban centers, the three partner organizations of the Urban Teacher Collaborative—Recruiting New Teachers, Inc. (RNT), the Council of Great City Schools (CGCS), and the Council of Great City Colleges of Education—conducted surveys of the urban schools and colleges of education in 1998–99. The results were published by the Urban Teacher Collaborative in the document "The Urban Teacher Challenge: Teacher Demand and Supply in the Great City Schools" (2000), available at the Council of Great City Schools' website at http://www.cgcs.org. The Great City Schools served 6.5 million students, of whom 40% were African-American; 30% Hispanic; 21% White; 6.4% Asian/ Pacific Islander; and 0.6% Alaskan/Native American. Just over 60% of students (60.5%) in the Great City Schools were eligible for free/reduced price lunch, 21% were English language learners, and 11.4% were students with individualized education programs (Urban Teacher Collaborative, 2000).

Great City school districts supplied information about their immediate and anticipated demand for teachers, recruitment strategies, and efforts to encourage diversity in the teacher workforce. Great City colleges of education provided information about their teacher preparation programs, subject areas of greatest interest to students, supports available to teacher preparation students, programs for nontraditional prospective teachers, and incentives and accommodations to attract applicants for high-need teaching areas (Urban Teacher Collaborative, 2000, p. 6). The surveys returned by districts and colleges of education updated information originally reported in the Urban Teacher Challenge in 1996, (Eubanks, 1996). That report, which provided a snapshot of teacher demand and preparation in Great City school districts and Great City colleges of education, asserted, "Without improved teacher recruitment and development processes this nation will fail to build the qualified, diverse, and culturally sensitive teacher workforce that today's and tomorrow's classrooms demand." (p. 17). This is still true today.

Recruitment strategies, excerpted from the Urban Teacher Challenge publication and reported by exemplary models, followed a pattern of use. All reported utilization of special recruitment efforts at colleges and universities as well as established partnerships with teacher education programs. With exception of one district, all reported that they recruited at historically black/Hispanic universities, offered induction support programs, sponsored job fairs to attract new teachers to school districts, offered Grow Your Own programs for students at elementary/middle/high school, and provided teacher academy and professional development activities. A few offered suggestions on streamlining the hiring process, retention strategies for minorities/diverse staff, induction programs and teacher orientation; a couple participated in international recruitment efforts, offered monetary bonus for talented and high-need subject area candidates, and tuition assistance for graduate course work. Only one reported offering incentives (e.g., housing assistance, relocation benefits, financial salary, waiving certain job/licensure requirements, school placement guarantees, provision of teacher employment information via a telephone hotline, and utilization of alternative licensure procedures, and assistance to out-of-state candidates).

The Urban Teacher Challenge survey (Urban Teacher Collaborative, 2000) asked districts whether targeted recruitment efforts were underway and, if so, what specific teacher recruitment strategies and procedures are employed.

Tables of Survey Data from Model Programs

Two tables are presented for the exemplary model program districts. Table 3.1 depicts the racial composition of teacher hires for the years 2004–2005 and 2005–2006. This snapshot of numbers and percentages of minority teacher hires during those two years was provided by AASPA member schools districts through survey data (Minority/Diverse Ad Hoc Committee survey). Table 3.2 was extracted from the AASPA survey devised by the author. Recruitment strategies are listed for the exemplary models, by district. This will give the reader an idea of the type of methods used in the recruitment effort. The instrument content was extracted from the Urban Teacher Challenge 2000 survey (Urban Teacher Collaborative, 2000).

Introduction to Models

Next you will find descriptions of exemplary minority recruitment models that work well in the featured school district and community. Readers may study each model and identify the methods, strategies, and programs that will work for their respective district situation. Information ranges from how to manage data of teachers hired to how to involve stakeholders— all focused on creating a successful minority teacher program. Contact information is noted for each district to provide immediate access to persons for further clarification about specifics of the program.

Following is a snapshot of selected model content from each district side by side. (See Figure 3.1.) This will provide an opportunity to see some similarities and differences at a glance. This study will enhance your knowledge of each model and its characteristics. Elements may vary from district to district since all school districts are unique in need;-what works for some may or may not work for others. The information is meant to pique interest in programs and strategies.

TABLE 3.1 Racial Composition for Total Hires

	Albemarle	Des Moines	Camera	Carrollton-Farmers	Lubbock
2004–2005					
Caucasion	88.2%	74.9%	79.5%	81.0%	82.0%
Black	6.8%	17.9%	19.4%	5.4%	7.0%
Hispanic	3.9%	5.1%	0.9%	12.2%	11.0%
Alaskan/Native American	0.0%	0.0%	0.0%	0.7%	0.0%
Asian/Pacific Islander	2.0%	2.1%	0.2%	0.7%	0.0%
2005–2006					
Caucasion	91.0%	83.0%	74.9%	73.6%	82.9%
Black	6.0%	12.6%	23.7%	10.5%	4.3%
Hispanic	1.0%	2.9%	1.1%	12.0%	11.5%
Alaskan/Native American	1.0%	0.1%	0.0%	0.5%	0.0%
Asian/Pacific Islander	1.0%	1.4%	0.3%	3.4%	1.3%

Source: Kearney-Gissendaner, J., for AASPA

TABLE 3.2 Teacher Recruitment Strategies By District

District	Special recruitment efforts at colleges and universities	Recruit at historically black/Hispanic colleges	International recruitment efforts	Incentives (e.g., housing assistance, relocation benefits, financial salary, etc.)	Waive certain job/licensure requirements	School placement guarantees	Offer on the spot contracts	Offer induction/support programs	Offer alternative certification routes	Offer monetary bonus for talented/high-need subject area candidates	Offer bonus for high student achievement	Offer loan forgiveness program	Tuition assistance for graduate course work	Incentives for NBPTS certification
Albemarle	•	•	•				•	•					•	•
CAMERA Consortium	•	•												
Carrollton-Farmers Branch	•	•	•					•	•					
Des Moines	•			•	•	•	•			•		•	•	
Lubbock	•	•						•		•		•		

	Model 1	Model 2	Model 3	Model 4
City or county residency requirement				
Provide guidance and information about teacher credentialing	•	•	•	•
Sponsor job fairs to attract new teachers to school district	•	•		•
Provide teacher employment information via telephone hotline				•
Participate in online counseling and/or job-finding services or Website	•			
Establish partnerships with teacher education programs	•	•	•	•
Streamline hiring process			•	•
Utilize alternative licensure procedures/assist out-of-state candidates			•	•
Establish searched for non-traditional teacherNon-traditional programs, I.e., Troops to Teacherss				
Non-traditional programs, i.e., Troops to Teachers	•		•	
Grow Your Own program for students in elementary/middle/high school	•	•	•	•
Retention strategies for minorities/diverse	•		•	•
Induction programs/teacher orientation			•	•
Teacher academy/Professional development activities	•		•	•
Other				•

FIGURE 3.1 At A Glance—Exemplary Minority Teacher Recruitment Teacher Models Information

Albemarle County	CAMERA	Carrollton Farmers	Des Moines	Lubbock

Three-pronged approach:
• Mentoring for Excellence
  Building Relationships
• Kids First
  Collaborative efforts
• Building Relationships
  Great Virginia Teach-In
	• Unique collaborative working relationship among districts
	• Beauty of program lies in simplicity
	• A "divvied up" process to identify every minority junior and senior
	• Grow Your Own programs in elementary, middle, and high school
		• Hosts job fairs with teacher teams, including principals
		• Participates in campus-level career fairs hosted by elementary and middle schools
		• Collaborative activities embracing teacher academies, Grow Your Own and induction programs
			• Teacher Quality Project (TQP)
			• Professional development schools
			• Partnerships with universities
			• Induction/support programs
				• Addresses student pipeline issues.
				• Targets colleges and universities with high minority enrollment in education.
				• Advisory committees.
				• Grow Your Own activities.
				• Hires juniors, seniors, and teaching assistants.
				• Time Release Program

The Albemarle County Public Schools Minority Recruitment Program

Albemarle County Public Schools, Charlottesville, VA
Contact: 434-296-5827

Background

The hiring of minority staff was a major need and focus area for the Albemarle human resources division. It was the philosophy and a goal of the division that the instructional staff should reflect the diversity of the student population. A priority of the school board and superintendent was to continue to make progress toward achieving this goal. These data indicate an increase in the overall number of minority teachers hired the first year of the program, from 14 to 18. This increase may be attributed to the ongoing commitment to diversity as a school system. Competition for minority candidates continued to be a challenge for the system as local competition from other systems and the location of Albemarle County made it challenging to recruit a more diverse population. For the counties surrounding Albemarle, minority recruitment, hiring, and retention continued to be a challenge.

Features of the Program

Mentoring for Excellence. In an effort to improve the county staff's diversity, the Albemarle County Schools partnered with the Charlottesville City Public Schools to develop better ways to attract and retain minority employees. An example of this collaboration is the Mentoring for Excellence program, which was created to provide cultural, personal, and professional coaching to new minority employees. Mentoring for Excellence was established in 2001 under the auspices of the human resources department and the superintendent's Equity and Diversity Committee. The mentors are leaders in the community who have volunteered to assist each new employee with their acclimation to their new position and the community. The mentor position was not designed to replace the building-level mentor, but to enhance the support provided. The success of the program, due in part to the support of the administration, was confirmed by the positive feedback received from the participants. Not only was there an increase in the diversity of the teacher participants, but there was also the largest number of educators involved since the program's inception. The program was advertised at Albemarle's New Teacher Academy and at the new employee orientations. Racial minorities have sought the program's support. Requests were also received from teachers with physical disabilities and other diverse needs. Corporate sponsors, Wachovia Bank and Real Estate III, hosted the program's end-of-the-year reception.

Building Relationships. Recruitment and retention go hand in hand. In an effort to attract and retain the best talent possible, a plan called Building Relationships was created to recruit instructional leaders to the division. In addition to the University of Virginia, five colleges and universities were identified and contacted in order to focus county resources to recruit and hire new employees from those schools. The decision on selecting the five schools was based on the following criteria:

- ◆ 5-year teacher programs (master's degree)
- ◆ graduating minority graduates
- ◆ graduating students with multiple endorsements
- ◆ graduates that possess multiple talents (e.g., coaching, sponsors)
- ◆ strong reputation for academic programs
- ◆ schools that have demographics similar to Albemarle County
- ◆ schools that have curriculum styles similar to Albemarle County (word study)

A team made up of human resources staff members, school administrators, and teachers was assigned to each college or university and was responsible for establishing rapport through presenting workshops for students in the education schools, meeting and collaborating on education and/or career development programs, and recruiting teacher candidates through the traditional means of a recruitment fair several times a year.

Kids First. Each year the school district hosted two onsite interviewing events called Kids First, a collaborative effort with three other local systems (Charlottesville City, Louisa County, and Orange County schools). Interviews were prearranged and the event typically took place the day before our State Recruitment Fair, the Great Virginia Teach-In. Three times a year the school division hosted social events called A Gathering of Folk. All diverse employees were invited to attend.

Action Plans. The district monitored programs by creating Action Plans for each program, completed by group efforts. Although individuals were assigned to specific areas of responsibilities, cross-functional teams completed each project.

Highlights of these successful programs include the following:

- ◆ an increase in the number of applications submitted
- ◆ an increase in the number of applicants who hold a degree higher than the bachelor's degree
- ◆ increases in the retention rates of minority employees

Evaluation

The success of the Building Relationships program was reported through the data of the Albemarle Human Resources Annual Report. This report contained student and employee ethnic distribution, teaching field demographics, newly employed teaching staff, and personal characteristics of new teaching staff. Evaluations for Kids First were completed by both program participants and interviewers. Evaluations were completed at the end of the school year for Mentoring for Excellence.

Organizational Culture

The culture of the school community had a significant impact on the district. Although the district location is in a relatively small community, it resides in the fourth largest county geographically in the State of Virginia. It had one of the highest cost-of-living indexes in the State, compared with Northern Virginia (the highest). The district's minority population was not significant, and this may have been a deterring factor in why minority professionals were not attracted to this community in large numbers. Due to the University of Virginia, the largest employer, the population was a transient one.

It is crucial to go beyond the traditional means when recruiting a diverse applicant pool and retaining employees. Oftentimes it takes a personal approach: meeting the family of the applicant, providing personal counseling and aligning ourselves with influential leaders in our community to network for us. Most of Albemarle County's diverse applicants find it by word of mouth.

Strategies

The district employed the following strategies to carry out the minority recruitment program:

- ◆ Special recruitment efforts at colleges and universities
- ◆ Recruit at historically black and Hispanic-serving colleges and universities
- ◆ International recruitment efforts
- ◆ Offer on-the-spot contracts (contingent upon a position reference)
- ◆ Offer induction/support programs
- ◆ Tuition assistance for graduate work
- ◆ Incentives for National Board Teachers (NBT)
- ◆ Provide guidance and information about teacher credentialing
- ◆ Sponsor job fairs to attract new teachers to our school district
- ◆ Participate in online counseling
- ◆ Establish partnerships with teacher education programs
- ◆ Nontraditional programs, for example, Troops to Teachers
- ◆ Grow Your Own programs
- ◆ Retention strategies for minorities and diversity
- ◆ Teacher Academy/Professional Development

Cleveland Area Minority Educators Recruitment Association (CAMERA)

Cleveland Area Minority Educators Recruitment Association, Cleveland, Ohio
Contact Information: 216-797-2905

Background

The Cleveland Area Minority Educators Recruitment Association (CAMERA), composed of Cleveland Municipal Schools and area districts, included nineteen districts working collaboratively to recruit quality teachers of color. These districts ranged from 99% minority to 99% majority student bodies, from under 2,500 to over 50,000 students. District officials identified every minority junior and senior education major attending the state's colleges of education.

A close look at the new hire statistics from the 2004–2005 and 2005–2006 school year showed that the first year over 21% of those hired were teachers of color, rising to 24% the second year. The teachers of color represented black, Hispanic, and Asian/Pacific Islanders. Although this percentage increase is still low, it represented progress in the Consortium's effort to recruit quality teachers of color.

Features of the Program

All state recruitment fairs were covered by CAMERA and relationships were built among college professors, college career officers, and CAMERA members. At historically black and minority college campuses, CAMERA relied on hired graduates to build an awareness of the program. Ohio credentialing is confusing at best, and CAMERA members were prepared to help future teachers understand this process. The area where the most help was given centered around the required Educational Testing Service (ETS) Praxis Tests that applicants must pass. Each district provided each selected student (prospective teacher) an overview of the consortium and the member districts. Each recruit could become a candidate for all districts by completing a very short application that was posted on a shared database and updated as listed candidates were selected for teaching positions.

Eventually the database contained 100 to 200 teacher candidates. All member districts, including those without student diversity, could interview minority candidates from the database.

A spring reception event attended by district representatives and the candidates allowed the candidates to gain a clearer understanding of the recruiting districts and to match their skills to district needs. At this event, the candidates had the opportunity to gain a better understanding of the recruiting districts and to match their skills with district needs.

For all new hires, the entry-year program was based at least partially on Ohio's adaptation of the ETS Praxis III program. Beyond the orientation to Praxis III, new teachers were involved in professional development activities specific to the instructional needs of the hiring district.

Evaluation

Evaluating success of the program varied from district to district. Some member districts had few or no minority students. Consequently, they had a more difficult time attracting minority educators. However, the consortium allowed them access to candidates whom they would never have had the opportunity to see without membership. Interviews of minority candidates increased in all districts. One outer-suburban/rural district was able to interview eight minority candidates for its seven open positions. Prior to CAMERA membership, this district had no minority candidates to interview.

Overall, success was measured by the number of candidates identified, interviewed, and hired each year. Since CAMERA is a recruiting consortium, retention was not rigorously measured, but the member districts expressed satisfaction with the quality and longevity of the hired candidates.

Organizational Culture

In regard to organizational culture and the program, the CAMERA members offered varied views and goals, a strong point as candidates could shop within the consortium to find those districts most closely meeting their needs and matching their styles. The program ensured that candidates were treated with respect and that the application process was minimized.

Some barriers to district efforts to attract and retain minority teachers were evident when offers were made by member districts that lacked diversity. Minority candidates, hoping for a more diverse setting, turned down offers. Although this was a natural consequence to be expected, introducing candidates to nondiverse member districts was of value within the overall mission of recruiting minorities.

Strategies

CAMERA members became familiar with college programs and worked to identify all minorities majoring in education. District members assumed responsibility for developing a good relationship with several of the state's colleges and supporting Future Educator Association (FEA) chapters in member districts. These FEA chapters encourage and support diverse membership and, therefore, are likely to send potential teachers to the partner colleges.

The strategies and related programs the CAMERA program used to enhance the recruitment program included the following:

- ◆ Special recruitment efforts at colleges and universities
- ◆ Recruiting at historically black/Hispanic-serving colleges
- ◆ Providing guidance and information about teacher credentialing

- ◆ Sponsoring job fairs to attract new teachers to school district
- ◆ Establishing partnerships with teacher education programs
- ◆ Implementing Grow Your Own program for students in elementary/middle/high school

As to retention, CAMERA had a no-compete rule in effect for the first year of a teacher's employment. If an offer was made by one member district, the other members agreed to refrain from making an offer unless the first offer was rejected.

Carrollton-Farmers Branch Independent School District Minority Recruitment Model

Carrollton-Farmers Branch, Texas
Contact Information: 972-968-6100

Background

The Carrollton-Farmers Branch Independent School District located in Texas aggressively sought minority applicants through a web-based application system and teacher job fairs both in and out of state. The district's goal was to hire and retain highly qualified minority teachers for a district of 26,000 students with an ethic breakdown of 47% Hispanic, 14.28% African American, 11.09% Asian, and 0.38% American Indian. During the 2004–2005 school year, they hired over 17% minority teachers, and during 2005–2006, over 25% minority teachers.

Features of the Program

The district contacted principals and encouraged them to set up interviews with prospective applicants. The personnel department also offered information and support to district paraprofessionals on the requirements to obtain a degree, or a teaching credential if they possessed a degree in education. Involving minority teachers and administrators in the recruitment process was reported as a positive factor, particularly at various teacher job fairs. Every administrator supported the idea of having minority teachers on all campuses to serve as positive role models for the minority/majority school district. Administrators of an ethnic group other than Caucasian actively sought the minority students and were instrumental in recruiting them for the district.

Job fairs were hosted each year with over 900 attendees. Principals brought teacher teams and interviewers on site the day of the job fair. The district efforts extended beyond attracting prospective applicants to the district. The personnel department participated in campus-level career fairs that the elementary and middle schools hosted each year. A flyer focusing on the concept of "What It Takes to Become a Teacher" and pencils with the logo, "Learn Today, Teach Tomorrow" were distributed to the students.

The personnel department visited education classes and future teacher groups of local universities such as the University of North Texas, Denton and Dallas campuses, Richland Community College, Brookhaven Community College, and Texas Women's University. Teachers for the district were recruited at the annual bilingual/ESL conference in the area. Personnel officials worked with paraprofessionals who wanted to pursue a teaching degree, sharing information with them regarding the Texas Educational Aide Exemption Program, whereby paraprofessionals who qualify can attend college and have their tuition costs paid. Paraprofessionals could have their student teaching requirement waived depending upon the number of years experience as an aide.

This Texas-sponsored program paid the tuition costs for instructional aides and required the individual to continue working as a classroom aide while attending college. The individual had to complete an application process in addition to submitting the FAFSA application. If the teacher assistant qualified, he or she was eligible to attend community college or university in pursuit of a teaching certificate or license. This program was under the direction of the Texas Higher Education Coordinating Board.

The district offered flex-time for paraprofessionals who need to take classes during the school day. Flex-time was given if the class was not offered in the evenings. Information was shared with a number of paraprofessionals who held degrees outside the field of education or from another country as to how to pursue a teaching certificate by going through an alternative certification program.

Carrollton-Farmers Branch personnel administrators served on the advisory board of four alternative certification programs: Region 10 Teacher Preparation and Certification Program, Education Career Alternatives Program, Richland Community College, and Brookhaven Community College Teacher Certification Program. Much collaboration took place between Carrollton-Farmer Branch ISD and these programs as well as other alternative certification programs in the pursuit to find minority applicants, particularly in the critical needs areas.

Using Title II funds, the district implemented a tuition/fee reimbursement program for teachers who were not fully certified and were pursuing full certification for their teaching assignment. During the 2005–2006 school year, Title II funds paid 100% of the reimbursement costs for sixty induction-year teachers. In addition to the Title II tuition/fee reimbursement program, the district's bilingual department offered classes for teachers pursuing certification in ESL. The department paid for the cost of the exam as well as the cost for adding this endorsement to their teaching credential.

The bilingual/ESL department hired university interns seeking a teaching degree to work as part-time ESL tutors. Many of these interns were minority students. Coordinators from the district's bilingual/ESL department had a very positive working relationship with bilingual/ESL university staff and assisted personnel in pursuit of teacher candidates. Bilingual teachers who were fully state-certified were given an annual stipend of $3,000. Induction-year teachers who were teaching in a bilingual classroom, but were not fully certified, were paid a $1,500 stipend.

Prospective bilingual teachers were treated to lunch when they came in to interview with principals, who then had the opportunity to answer questions about the district as well as establish a positive rapport. As a recruiting tool, the program advertised the fact that teachers may have opportunities for their university student loans to be deferred and/or cancelled as a result of working on a Title I campus. There are twenty-seven Title I schools in Carrollton-Farmer's total of thirty-eight campuses. A list of other perks awarded to teachers follows.

◆ Chamber of Commerce solicited in-kind donations from businesses in the area to give to teachers.
◆ Door prizes were donated by local businesses.
◆ All teachers received a computer, printer, and Presentation Station equipped with a document camera, a data projector, a DVD player, PowerPoint, and a Classroom Performance System for their classroom teaching.
◆ During the 2006–2007 school year, all teachers received an iPod. This is an initiative called Beyond 4 Walls whereby teachers are both consumers and producers. Teachers will have access to video and audio podcasts to enhance instruction in the classroom.

Evaluation

The district measured success by the number of minority teachers retained each year and also by the number of first-year teachers that secured their state certification by the end of the school year. Certification progress of each teacher was tracked throughout the school year until they secured their teaching credential. Data were kept on the number of applicants seen at the teacher job fairs throughout the year, and the ethnicity of each applicant was noted.

Each semester, documentation from the Texas Higher Education Coordinating Board concerning paraprofessional participation in the Educational Aide Exemption Program was received. For the 2005–2006 school year, eleven paraprofessionals were working toward their teaching degrees as a result of this state-sponsored program. Ten teacher assistants were involved in this program.

The district tracked and maintained records of the number of teachers submitting documentation (receipts) for reimbursement costs through the tuition/fee reimbursement program—an ongoing process. Personnel officials worked closely with principals and teachers in an effort to retain minority teachers.

Organizational Culture

The district/organizational culture affected the program through many activities ensuring that everyone felt welcome to the school, district, and the community. Below is a list of what this school district offered:

◆ The district's Educational Foundation awarded $100 to each induction-year teacher to assist with classroom supplies and materials.

◆ The Foundation awarded innovative grants up to $1,000 to teachers through an application process twice during the school year.

◆ A luncheon, sponsored by the Metrocrest Chamber of Commerce, was held during the summer for all new professional employees hired for the new school year. The children of employees could attend Carrollton-Farmers Branch schools regardless of whether the parent resided in the district or in that attendance zone.

◆ All new hires were required to attend a teacher academy prior to the start of school and were paid $50 a day for their attendance. First-year teachers were required to complete five days while veteran teachers attended three days.

◆ The personnel department offered free prep classes for teachers who were scheduled to take the state-required exams to obtain certification. Prep sessions were offered for the content and pedagogy exams.

◆ A manual for the 2006–2007 school year for teacher assistants and clerical staff included how to have transcripts translated and evaluated and descriptions of the Educational Aide Exemption Program and alternative certification programs and universities.

◆ Spanish classes Level I and II were offered to teachers who wanted to learn the language or improve their skills.

◆ "The Applause Card" offered discounts and incentives to all employees. Discounts ranged from restaurant to apartment to investment services. The program was sponsored by the Chamber of Commerce from the cities of Farmers Branch, Greater Irving-Las Colinas, and the Metrocrest as well as the district's Educational Foundation.

◆ All employees received an Employee Activity Card. It allowed employees and immediate family members to attend football games and theatre/musical productions free of charge.

The following are some barriers the Carrollton-Farmers Branch Independent School District faced in attracting and retaining minority teachers. The district is located in the Dallas-Ft.Worth Metroplex and the demand for minority teachers is high for every district in the area. There were not enough minorities going into the field of education in order to keep up with the demand. Some of the larger districts offered incentives such as signing bonuses, relocation allowance, and annual bilingual stipends larger than what Carrollton-Farmers Branch offered ($3,000), which did not pay a signing bonus or relocation allowance.

There was competition within the area with beginning teacher salaries. Teachers, particularly those new to the profession, now "shop the market" for the best starting salary. Starting salaries in the Dallas Ft. Worth Metroplex ranged from $44,255 to $41,200, with the average being $42,038. Carrollton-Farmers Branch salary for first-year teachers was $41,500.

Housing costs in the Carrollton area were substantially higher than the rapidly growing communities of Allen, McKinney, and Frisco. Once teachers purchase homes in these new communities because it is less expensive, they secure jobs with these school districts since the drive from these communities to Carrollton-Farmers Branch becomes rather frustrating due to the traffic and distance.

Strategies

The following strategies were used to develop the Carrollton-Farmers Branch program:

◆ The primary strategy used was to actively and aggressively pursue minority applicants either through an online application system or through attending teacher job fairs. The district offered contracts to applicants the spring semester prior to the new school year in an effort to build up a pool of minority teachers.

♦ Personnel officials pursued student teachers who had completed their internship and offered them contracts for the upcoming school years. If they completed their internship during the fall semester, personnel administrators encouraged them to work as substitute teachers for the district during the spring semester.

♦ As principals became aware of paraprofessionals on their campuses, who were either working on their education degree or were seeking an alternative certification route, they encouraged them to continue their pursuit. Principals asked these individuals to contact the personnel office for information on how to become a teacher. The principal likely was planning to hire that individual for their campus once certification was completed.

♦ District paraprofessionals who became teachers and were hired by the district as teachers were reported to be some of the most loyal employees. Most of the time they already lived in the district and had done so for many years. Their children attended Carrollton-Farmers Branch schools. This is why the district encourages paraprofessionals to seriously consider the state's

Des Moines Public School District Minority Recruitment Model

Teacher Quality Project, Des Moines, Iowa
Contact: 515-633-5038

Background

During the school years 2004–2005 and 2005–2006, the Des Moines Public School District (DMPS), Iowa, hired over 500 teachers in each school year. Of those teachers hired, minority hires approached and exceeded 20% of total hires.

Through a federal grant awarded in 2005, in partnership with Drake University, a four-year private college with a teacher education program, and Des Moines Area Community College (DMACC), a two-year public junior college, DMPS recruited minority teacher education candidates, provided access to higher education leading to teacher certification, placed successful candidates in DMPS teaching positions, and supported them with mentors and professional development. The goal of the Teacher Quality Project (TQP) was to increase the number of highly qualified teachers of color serving students in the DMPS.

Features of the Program

The TQP program gained momentum with over one hundred applications, three times the numbers that had been received in past years. A solid infrastructure and agreement about procedures to recruit and select candidates had been established among the TQP's partners, Des Moines Area Community College (DMACC) and Drake University. Additionally, principals expressed interest in mentoring teacher candidates and providing staff development for their enrichment opportunities.

The TQP used a holistic approach to recruiting strategies, since research indicates that recruiting and retention must be addressed together. Supports were provided so that minority teacher candidates succeeded in higher education and stayed in the district as teachers.

First, to attract potential teachers, several recruiting strategies were used, including Grow Your Own recruitment of DMPS employees, community connection and involvement, and traditional media, for example, newspaper advertisements.

Second, financial support (based on student needs) enabled potential candidates to gain access to higher education through scholarships and forgivable loans. TQP teachers were forgiven one year of loans for each year they taught for the DMPS.

Third, professional support was provided to make the higher education experience as smooth as possible. Advisors served as one point of contact for TQP students at each college, for academic, business, and financial needs. Based on the result of a needs survey, mentoring and cohort experience was provided.

Finally, the transition from teacher education student to teacher was supported when new teachers were mentored by district teachers for three years, rather than the usual two years; professional development was provided to assist TQP teachers; and teachers were assisted in meeting the qualifications of a "highly qualified teacher."

Evaluation

The success of the TQP was evaluated by meeting the goals of the grant: to increase the number of quality minority teachers in the Des Moines Public Schools' classrooms to serve students best. The TQP program recruited, trained, supported, and retained minority candidates, including Native Americans, who were interested in teaching.

Stakeholders met to determine to what extent the criteria, benchmarks, and timelines specified in the grant were being met. The district provided documentation of the efforts to address these criteria and benchmarks. For example, TQP student schedules showing science and math courses were submitted to the grant agency.

Des Moines Public School District officials emphasized that standard recruiting activity with a focus on recruiting minority teaching candidates had been in operation for many years. The district received a federal grant in 2005 that enhanced and supported a district-designed program targeting the recruitment of minority teaching candidates.

Organizational Culture

The goal of the TQP to assist new minority teachers in feeling welcome through the creation of community effort began with recruiting and continued throughout the new teacher's induction into the district and school. Principals were trained to implement welcome receptions using induction activities including tours of the new teachers' classrooms and introductions to colleagues. Stereotypes of Iowa lifestyles sometimes interfered with successful recruiting and retaining of minority teachers. Often times out-of-state teacher candidates could harbor negative perceptions of the extreme cold weather and the lack of diversity in a community. Minority teacher candidates do not want to move to places that isolate them from family and friends. But it was noted that once in Des Moines, most minority teachers were fine. To address any barriers, the TQP provided cultural sensitivity and competency training to address skills teachers needed to cope with different cultures.

The ability to finance the college coursework needed to attain a teaching degree presented a barrier to minority teacher prospects. The TQP provided financial information to potential teacher candidates so that they could make informed decisions. Financial aid, scholarships, and forgivable loans were made available to qualifying candidates. All candidates could apply for financial aid so that support was provided from all sources. Prospective teachers represented different educational and financial backgrounds. Some already possessed the bachelor degree, which was helpful in reducing the content area of required courses, and having a current job assisted in paying tuition.

While not perceived as a barrier, there was a requirement that teachers who completed the program and were hired by DMPS must teach in the district one year for each year they had a forgivable loan.

Strategies

The following strategies were used to carry out the minority recruitment program:

- ◆ Special recruitment efforts at colleges and universities
- ◆ Incentives (e.g., housing assistance, relocation benefits, financial, salary)
- ◆ Waive certain job/licensure requirements
- ◆ School placement guarantees
- ◆ Offer induction/support programs
- ◆ Offer monetary bonus for talented/high-need subject area candidates

- ◆ Offer loan forgiveness program
- ◆ Tuition assistance for graduate course work
- ◆ Provide guidance and information about teacher credentialing
- ◆ Establish partnerships with teacher education programs
- ◆ Streamline hiring process
- ◆ Establish searches for nontraditional teachers
- ◆ Nontraditional programs, i.e., Troops to Teachers
- ◆ Retention strategies for minorities/diverse Teacher academy/professional development activities

Lubbock Independent School District Minority Recruitment Program

Lubbock Independent School District, Texas
Contact: 806-766-1138

Background

The Lubbock Independent School District, located in northwest Texas, had a minority recruitment program with outstanding key components to successfully recruit quality candidates. Over 18% of teacher hires in the 2004–2005 school year were minorities. Of those 18%, 11% were Hispanic, and 7% black. For the 2005–2006 school year, similar percentages were reported with over 16% minorities hired (11.5% Hispanic, 4.3% Black, 1.3% Asian).

Features of the Program

Personnel officials reported having high school juniors and seniors hired by the district to work as teaching assistants during the school day in the primary grades to introduce them to the world of teaching. Other program components include the following:

♦ Targeting colleges and universities that have high minority enrollment in their college of education programs.

♦ Training and placing student teachers on campuses with high minority enrollment in order to offer these college students an opportunity to work with diverse groups.

♦ Working closely with local junior colleges. Support is provided for teacher assistants to attend college-sponsored seminars. The district officials work individually with the teacher assistants to answer questions about the teaching profession.

♦ Tracking minority candidates who apply for teacher assistant positions, and have completed some college coursework. The district allowed for release time during the work day. Teacher assistants could attend college classes as many as 10 hours per week during work days.

♦ Provision of summer school positions to teacher assistants seeking a degree to assist them financially.

♦ Formulation of a Minority Recruitment Advisory Committee composed of district personnel as well as local citizens. The committee addressed strategies to bring minority groups into teacher preparation programs.

♦ Proactive hiring of non-degreed as well as degreed individuals outside of education to encourage them to pursue teaching as a career. As a result, the district hired these individuals as teacher assistants and brought them in on a higher pay scale than other teacher assistants to further encourage them to seek teaching as a career.

♦ Endorsement of the Texas Educational Aide Exemption Program was a major component to expand the pool of prospective teachers. This Texas-sponsored program paid the tuition costs for instructional aides who worked in classrooms while attending college. If the teacher assistant qualified, he or she was eligible to attend either a community college or university in pursuit of a teaching certificate. All applicants for

Lubbock's teacher assistant positions received information about this program and about college teacher preparation programs.

◆ The Time Release Program was one of the most successful projects especially for the teacher assistant working to gain a bachelor of science degree through a teacher preparation program or for the individual in the last year or semester of work. Universities began to offer more classes after the 4:00 p.m. hour as opposed to only offering classes during the workday.

◆ Another successful feature is hiring these individuals as teacher assistants and paying them at a higher pay rate. Since many of these assistants have families, this feature provides financial assistance while they are pursuing their degree.

◆ Many of the program's teacher assistants had degrees and were post-baccalaureate students pursuing their teacher certification. They were acquiring an extraordinary amount of classroom experience. On the average, an individual in this situation only lacks 12 to 15 hours of education coursework.

Organizational Culture

People were welcomed to the school, district, and community. For example, the personnel office worked diligently to attract applicants from other communities. When an applicant came in, they were made to feel comfortable. Strong candidates were invited to visit the district with expenses paid (e.g., hotel stays, airfare, and mileage fees). These candidates visited campuses and interview with principals. Local and Title funds were used for this recruitment effort. The superintendent's offices as well as the school board were supportive of having a diverse teaching staff.

The most obvious barrier to the district efforts to attract and retain minority teachers was the lack of minority teachers entering the profession nationwide. In Texas, everyone is fighting to get the same teachers. In the Lubbock area, there is a high Hispanic population, but not a large African-American population, unlike metropolitan areas of Texas.

Strategies

The following strategies were used to carry out Lubbock's minority recruitment program:

- Special recruitment efforts at colleges and universities
- Recruit at historically Black/Hispanic-served colleges
- Offer induction/support programs
- Offer monetary bonus for talented/high-need subject area candidates
- Offer loan forgiveness program
- Provide guidance and information about teacher credentialing
- Sponsor job fairs to attract new teachers to school district
- Provide teacher employment information via telephone hotline
- Establish partnerships with teacher education programs
- Streamline hiring process
- Utilize alternative licensure procedures/assist out-of-state candidates
- Grow Your Own program for students in elementary/middle/high school
- Retention strategies for minorities
- Induction programs/teacher orientation
- Teacher academy/professional development activities
- A Grow Your Own effort was the most productive form of minority recruitment, and as a result, a great amount of emphasis was placed on this local effort. That the district recruits from within, from high school students to their teacher assistants, was considered a strong asset to the program.

Summary

These exemplary models represent outstanding minority teacher recruitment practices that are being shared by dedicated human resource and personnel officials of the American Association of School Personnel Association (AASPA) membership. Their work goal can inspire members to build similar programs in their districts and organizations to make a difference in hiring larger numbers and percentages of minority teachers for our nation's diverse student body.

For the years 2004–2005 and 2005–2006, minority teachers were more than 10% of all teachers hired in these districts, and most of the districts reported that minorities approached 20% of teachers hired. These percentages indicate that certain dynamics with their program plan were working together to produce positive results. Of the 29 recruitment strategies listed from "The Urban Teacher Challenge" (Urban Teacher Collaborative, 2000) recruitment strategy chart, at least one of the five exemplary model programs utilized all strategies listed with exception of two: a) offering bonuses for high school student achievement, and b) requiring a city or county residency requirement.

Let us examine characteristics and factors of the five model districts that determined their success. Important lessons have been learned from these model programs. Maintaining data on minority hires each year regarding number of hires and percentages and the strategies used to operate the minority recruitment program serve to shed light on both successes and needed improvements.

The model descriptions have provided insightful information on how each district handled the challenge of locating, recruiting, selecting, hiring, and maintaining a minority teacher recruitment force. Each district had distinct features, yet very similar strategies and operations. It is clear that certain strategies were foundations of excellent minority teacher recruitment and most always were found in each district. They are the following:

- ◆ **Recruitment at historically black colleges and universities**
  Albemarle County School District personnel officials focused their recruitment efforts here; established partnerships with teacher education programs; and collaborated by using a three-pronged approach targeting precollegiate, college, paraprofessionals, and career changers.

◆ **Special recruitment efforts at colleges and universities**
The CAMERA program (Cleveland Municipal Schools and area districts) had a unique teacher recruitment program inclusive of nineteen districts working collaboratively to recruit quality teachers of color" from the state's colleges of education.

◆ **Sponsored job fairs to attract new teachers to school district**
Carrollton-Farmers Branch Independent School District hosts job fairs each year. Principals participate with teacher teams and interview on site on the job fair days. Their efforts extend beyond attracting prospective applicants to the district. The personnel department participates in campus level career fairs that their elementary and middle schools host each year.

◆ **Provision of guidance and information about teacher credentialing**
CAMERA progam believes that the beauty of their program lies in its simplicity. They feel that they make it "easy" for minorities to apply. And they share information freely and in a non-competitive atmosphere.

◆ **Establishment of partnerships with teacher education programs**
CAMERA's recruitment program is described by the district's officials as a "divvied up" process of the state's colleges of education where they work to identify every minority junior and senior education major.

◆ **Grow Your Own program for students in elementary/ middle/high schools**
CAMERA program maintains this to be a major focus, for students at each grade level; Des Moines introduces middle and high school students to careers in teaching; Lubbock personnel officials hire high school juniors and seniors to work as teaching assistants during the school day in the primary grades in the elementary schools. This activity introduces the students to the "world of teaching."

- ◆ **Teacher academy/professional development activities**
  Des Moines has a Teacher Quality Project (TQP) that includes working with professional development schools, partnerships with universities, community colleges in recruiting minority teacher education candidates.
- ◆ **Some type of induction/support programs**
  Carrollton-Farmers Branch personnel administrators are highly involved in collaborative activities embracing teacher academies, "Grow Your Own," and induction programs.

The author challenges the reader to share this research and valuable information to build an effective minority recruitment and retention model for an organization or school district.

4

Pipeline Programs for Minority Teacher Recruitment

Grow Your Own: Pipeline Programs

Pipeline programs are programs that build bridges and partnerships with communities locally, statewide, and nationally to recruit quality teachers focused on minority and diverse staff. These partnerships are built with the communities, agencies, churches, universities, and businesses that are interested in locating prospective teachers. Such programs begin at the elementary, middle, and high school building level in a Grow Your Own program. These programs are identified as Educators of Tomorrow, Future Educators Association (FEA), and Future Teachers Association (FTA). These programs build a base for statewide and nationwide programs seeking prospective teachers.

The teacher recruitment models discussed in preceding chapters have many dimensions of these pipeline programs that may be incorporated into local Grow Your Own recruitment programs. Ideas may be applied to current situations, using new strategies that will assist you in finding adequate numbers of minority/diverse staff and other teachers needed to staff your schools. In other words, energize into a new Grow Your Own recruiting strategy! These strategies invest in district-connected people. School boards of education, if informed about these programs, will realize dollar savings by using the pipeline program to recruit as will traditional recruitment on college campuses. This new paradigm gives meaning to old ideas!

The Grow Your Own recruitment strategy for today's environment is now workable in a new concept. In chapter 1, the author discussed Dr. Martin Haberman's research that substantiated the rationale for recruiting and preparing adults as teachers of diverse children in urban poverty; and these pipeline programs target such persons (Haberman, 2005, p. 23).

The next chapters will provide information concerning the type of pipeline programs you may consider in building Grow Your Own recruitment strategies. These feature programs at the school-building level, Grow Your Own statewide-level participation (e.g. Council Attracting Prospective Educators, known as CAPE); Grow Your Own partnerships (e.g., Northland Teacher Academy; Project Toolkit; BECOME program, South Carolina Teacher Cadet Program); and the Ohio Department of Education Initiatives of the New Teacher Project partnership in Ohio urban districts. Ohio Core initiatives and Troops to Teachers are additional resources to consider to keep the pipeline of teachers flowing.

Grow Your Own Recruitment Strategies

The Grow Your Own recruitment strategy is not a new phenomenon to educators and human resource officials. Many school districts across the nation have developed some form of this model to identify students who are interested in the field of teaching and education. These programs, in conjunction with teacher recruitment programs, help in combating teacher shortages, especially the lack of minority teachers in the classrooms. But the key to the success of these programs in identifying future teachers and having them come back to respective districts to teach lies in how well a local district nurtures the pipeline of prospective teachers.

A Grow Your Own program may begin as an elementary, middle, and high school level program targeting students who may be interested in becoming a future teacher. In the simplest form, the school district may create an extra-duty position to coordinate an educator-of-tomorrow program. Teachers who are interested must be committed to recruiting youth into teaching, see students' strengths, nurture them, and work with them in establishing a future teacher program. Principals must be responsible to oversee and provide support for this program.

Example of a District Grow Your Own Program

An Ohio district Grow Your Own program includes the following components:

1. A strong service program for children in grades K-4. The children help with room and building tasks and projects, read to and tutor younger children, go to care facilities for people of all ages and read to them, interact with them, and perform for them (singing and musical instruments).

2. When children reach the fifth grade, principals help organize Future Educators of America (FEA) chapters. The FEA chapter members work on school service projects, recognize their teachers by preparing breakfasts for them, read to younger children; read to and help persons in the care facilities, and so on. Students also do neighborhood clean-up projects, go to a store and buy foods for shut-ins, and assist teachers in their rooms.

3. As students go to middle school, they continue in their FEA chapter and engage in service activities. They are encouraged to visit a college or university and learn about college life and career opportunities. Students could also go to a college and learn about future CAPE (Council Attracting Prospective Educators) summer opportunities to explore teaching as a career.

4. In grades 9 to 12, students continue to participate in service projects, in Future Educators of America (FEA) chapters, and work as volunteers. Students may continue to broaden their experiences in service learning and projects by helping younger children and high school students who need help in academic areas. Students may continue in FEA chapter work. When students go in to grades 11 and 12, they may participate in urban and/or local school districts' career and technical programs that prepare future teachers. (There are well over 135 such programs in Ohio.)

They may also participate in Ohio Future Educators of America (OFEA) state-wide meetings regarding teacher prep projects. There are also opportunities to attend National FEA conferences.

5. After high school, students may go to college to take teacher licensure prep programs in many areas of teaching. They will have opportunities to return to their home school districts and participate in classroom field experiences for credit as well as student teaching.

After receiving their college degrees and licenses, they could return to their school districts to teach—thus, the Grow Your Own program. To ensure that students come back to your districts to teach, an agreement may be written as such to track these students and develop a partnership with area colleges and universities to make that a reality.

These components of Grow Your Own are operating successfully in a number of states and with support of various organizations, for example, Columbus Educators of Tomorrow. Responsibilities of this type of program may include and are not limited to creating a steering committee (administrator, teacher counselor, PTA representative, student community representative), recruiting and identifying students from each grade level, offering workshop activities during the school year, developing a calendar of events for the future teacher program, and coordinating, marketing, and publicizing the program.

Ohio Future Educators Association

An example of a state organization is OFEA (Ohio Future Educators Association), a dynamic statewide organization for middle school and high school youth who are interested in a career in education. It was initiated in 1991 by the Ohio Department of Education and Phi Delta Kappa, an honor society for professional educators, and is growing every year.

OFEA works with advisors and officers of local chapters to recruit members and plan projects and activities; provide information about trends and programs for future educators; and provide statewide communication for advisors and members.

OFEA helps to motivate students who are interested in a career in education by encouraging them to: 1) set educational and career goals early in life, 2) focus on academic achievement, 3) explore teaching through direct experience in classrooms, and 4) become citizen leaders through service to their schools and communities.

OFEA has a state executive committee consisting of both students and advisors elected at the spring convention. OFEA officers must be students. The committee members plan the conference agenda, prepare and distribute a statewide newsletter, and represent Ohio at the National FEA convention.

The mission of OFEA is to 1) strengthen local chapters, 2) interest middle and high school youth in a career in education, 3) promote scholarship and academic excellence in local chapters, 4) develop and nurture qualities and aptitudes basic to effective teaching, 5) foster an understanding of the role of teachers, 6) make students aware of career opportunities in education; 7) help students reach their goals of becoming teachers, 8) encourage hands-on classroom teaching experiences in local chapters, 9) help students develop civic leadership skills through service to their community, and 10) encourage students to develop innovative ideas in education.

Ohio statistics provide us with the following (OFEA brochure, n.d.):

- More than 112,000 teachers are employed in Ohio schools each year.
- The number of Ohio teaching vacancies is rising due to large numbers of teacher retirements and increased enrollments, leading to the need for additional schools, classrooms, and teachers.
- Schools report a great need for special education teachers as well as middle school and adolescent/ young adult teachers in the fields of science mathematics, and foreign languages.

Fifty higher education institutions in Ohio offer programs leading to teacher licensure, including 13 public universities and 37 private colleges or universities.

Future Educators of America

Another effective program is the Future Educators of American (FEA). Originally known as Future Teachers of America, the FEA was once sponsored by the National Education Association and then the Association of Teacher Educators. During this time, it was renamed the Future Educators of America. In 1994, sponsorship shifted to PDK International. To more accurately reflect the international nature of the organization, PDK changed the name to Future Educators Association in 2005.

Through efforts to provide students with the most relevant opportunities to investigate what it means to be a teacher, FEA offers two distinct programs for prospective educators: a precollegiate level, referred to as FEA, and a collegiate level, known as FEA Professional. The association is unique in its ability to offer students unparalleled, age-appropriate professional development opportunities, including an annual conference and access to a state-of-the-art FEA social networking website. Through hands-on career exploration opportunities, FEA allows members to assume leadership roles and develop professional skill sets that will serve them throughout their careers. The association also connects students with chances to earn scholarship grants through PDK International.

The FEA program not only benefits its members but also has long-lasting, positive impact on our nation's school systems. By attracting exemplary candidates to the teaching profession, especially those from diverse cultural and ethnic backgrounds, FEA will directly influence an increase in qualified teachers. The work of FEA will elevate the image of teaching and promote it as a challenging and rewarding career.

FEA (Future Educator Association) chapters may be started by one committed individual—a student, a teacher, a business leader, a school administrator, a parent—to light the spark. That individual contacts others who see a need for a Future Educators of America chapter. As a group, these individuals examine their local needs, discuss how they believe a chapter can help them meet those needs, and begin to involve students in initial planning and organization. The next step is to contact Phi Delta Kappa and request an organizational manual. Organizers may write or call: Phi Delta Kappa, 408 North Union, Bloomington, IN 47405-3800. Phone (812) 339-1156 or 1-800-766-1156.

Ohio Minority Recruitment Consortium (OMRC)

A statewide Grow Your Own program is the Ohio Minority Recruitment Consortium (OMRC), a standing committee of the Ohio Association of School Personnel Administrators. Its one overarching goal is to provide its members with the tools they need to meet the challenges of diversity in Ohio's schools. Ohio's student population is becoming more diverse, yet the state's teaching force is becoming less diverse. OMRC works with administrators and districts to address this imbalance by sharing proven strategies for recruiting educators of color.

OMRC is a forum for interested public school districts, colleges, universities, private schools, community and state agencies, and individuals who are interested in the issues of diversity in its schools, the achievement gaps between students of color and white students, and the Ohio Department of Education standards for teachers. OMRC helps its members in many other ways, including support of the annual Council Attracting Prospective Educators (CAPE) Academy and the Council for Attracting and Retaining Educators (CARE) workshop. The consortium also works with the Ohio Department of Education, Phi Delta Kappa, and Future Educators of America to enlarge the pools of people of color candidates for teaching positions.

The Grow Your Own concept has been recognized nationally as Ramirez, of *US News and World Report* (Ramirez, 2007) noted that many of the best candidates already live in the neighborhood. But, far too often, persons that aspire to become teachers lack the credentials. He explained that many teachers-to-be have worked as teacher assistants, mentors, or volunteers in the classroom, but have not completed their college degrees. These persons, though, had the abilities to teach bilingual students since they were natives of other countries. He noted that, today, these women are "just the type of teachers the city's schools are looking for." School districts officials are weary of first-year teachers who "flee" to suburban schools, and Illinois is spending $7.5 million to help individuals described in the article to become teachers in underperforming schools in neighborhoods like their own. The initiative of Grow Your Own in Illinois aims to prepare 1,000 such teachers by 2016. Candidates, mostly women of color from low-income communities, receive forgivable college loans of up to $25,000 in exchange for a minimum five-year commitment to teach in underserved schools.

According to Ramirez (2007), similar initiatives have sprouted in urban school districts across the country. In Broward County, Florida, schools give college scholarships and guarantee jobs to high school students who return as certified teachers. In Seattle, the emphasis is on developing teachers from immigrant groups, while schools in Long Beach, California, work with local colleges to produce teachers in the hard-to-staff areas of science and math (pp. 1–2). Further, Ramirez stated that the success of such programs hinges on funding from private donors and the state and ongoing collaboration among neighborhood groups, universities, and school districts that work as teams to recruit, train, and place teachers in classrooms. For the candidates, the biggest challenge is juggling the responsibilities of schoolwork, jobs, and family life.

The Grow Your Own programs have the potential to produce a cadre of teachers for your respective district if follow-up is completed, support is provided by the district officials, and further work is completed to link your building Grow Your Own program to state programs, university partnerships, and teacher academies that produce teachers exclusively for the local community.

Three Pipeline Program Profiles

The three programs described below are included to provide detailed information on successful programming and strategies that interface with each other to provide a "pipeline" of support for future teachers. Each program represents steps in the process in identifying, nourishing, and guiding interested persons in choosing teaching as a career. A major focus is placed on addressing diversity and forming partnerships to "grow your own" in your own back yard.

The following, Council Attracting Prospective Educators (CAPE), is reprinted from AASPA Perspective, 2008, pp. 16–17, "From Camp to Academy: A Grow Your Own Ohio Model" written by the author, Janet E. Kearney-Gissendaner, Ph.D.

Council Attracting Prospective Educators (CAPE)

Overview of CAPE

The Ohio Council Attracting Prospective Educators (CAPE) program is a unique strategy for Growing Teachers, and it is working for Ohio! This strategy was modeled after a Phi Delta Kappa program that targets ways to recruit teachers of color. It was developed by a group of concerned personnel leaders as a means of diversifying the teaching force across Ohio. Grow Your Own programs are set up in elementary, middle and high schools to actively encourage prospective minority students to enter the field of education. A strong, supportive team meets during the year to plan dynamic programs to meet Ohio's need for diversifying the teaching force. The CAPE Board of Directors represents a cross section of interested people: personnel officials, college/university educators, administrators, Ohio Department of Education officials, Ohio Board of Regents staff, and retired educators. The CAPE program is supported by the Ohio Department of Education and the Ohio Minority Recruitment Consortium (OMRC).

From camp to academy

For over fourteen years (1992–2005), CAPE summer camps were held at selected colleges/university locations throughout Ohio. The host sites included large and small private. Over the years, approximately 740 high school students participated in the summer camps. After high school graduation, several hundred of these students entered a college or university to pursue a degree in education and become a teacher. Our program survey data indicate that approximately 76% of these students are now teachers in Ohio schools or in colleges or universities studying to be teachers—a very impressive record. In 1996, a second CAPE program was added. The program is entitled Council Attracting and Retaining Educators (CARE). CARE is a summer workshop scholarship program for students who attended CAPE summer camps and are now in colleges or universities preparing to be classroom teachers. Each scholarship is worth $500.00.

The Council for Prospective Educators (CAPE) has moved to Academy status. After fourteen years of CAPE summer camps, a review of the program was completed by the CAPE Steering Committee and Ohio Department of Education to update and ensure quality for future summer programs. A CAPE summer program was not offered in 2006 to allow time for this work to be completed. After extensive work, the camp concept was replaced with a new program. The new CAPE was now recognized as CAPE Teacher Academy. The CAPE Teacher Academy features a five-day summer academy at a selected Ohio university designed to provide an awareness of teaching and/or professional education as a career and to provide exposure to campus life. While the participants are typically rising juniors and seniors from high schools throughout the state of Ohio, participants for this first year also included a rising sophomore and one recently graduated senior. The goal of CAPE is to identify and attract talented young people from diverse backgrounds to careers in teaching while placing an emphasis on increasing the number of teachers of color and retaining them in teaching; diversity of the participants is of utmost importance. CAPE Academy participants are selected on the basis of academic record, activities, honors, application materials, and expressed interest in teaching as a career. The first CAPE Teacher Academy was held at the University of Dayton on June 18–22, 2007. There were 41 participants who were predominately female (83%), in either tenth or eleventh grade (96%), and almost evenly split between white (49%) and persons of color (51%). Accomplished Academy goals and objectives included the following:

◆ Refinement and customization of previously developed and implemented CAPE programs and schedules to provide participating students with instruction from CAPE faculty, selected University of Dayton faculty and guest speakers to further emphasize the professional assessments for beginning teachers. The content domains included: A) organizing content knowledge for student learning, B) creating an environment for student learning, C) teaching for student learning, and D) teacher professionalism. The Ohio Standards for the teaching professional were also introduced to develop knowledge and skills inclusive in the instructional process.

◆ Access to historical exhibits (Paul Dunbar Home) to extend cultural understanding of an international poet and his exhibits of literary treasures that depict social dilemmas of his day which gave rise to proclamation of black dignity.

The refined and customized CAPE schedule was rich with activities designed to expose participants to teaching as a profession with an emphasis on 1) Praxis and Pathwise Principles and Domains (including issues surrounding assessment vs. evaluation, student learning, classroom environment professionalism, curriculum, and lesson planning); 2) acquiring leadership skills and public speaking skills; 3) role model educators; 4) creativity enhancement activities; 5) problem-solving skills; 6) teacher preparation programs; 7) campus life; 8) developing portfolios (presented by the Greene County Career Center); 9) Ohio college fair; and 10) career possibilities.

Highlights of the five-day residential campus experience included five or six daily instructional blocks of varying lengths, daily faculty meetings with a small group of participants and a CAPE staff member, and large group sessions with dynamic speakers to energize students. College/university, CAPE faculty, and other guest presentations were presented, and cultural and recreational activities, both on and off campus, were enjoyed by all. A popular activity was the student participation in a mock job interview to provide early insight on expectations during an authentic interview. Students were prepared for the interview by CAPE instructors, including how to dress for success. Also present was the Ohio Teacher of the Year for 2006, Eric Combs, who presented a powerful speech on the topic, "Extending Student Thinking Skills."

An evaluation of the 2007 Academy focused on attendees' perceptions of the program and how much the experience affected their desire to pursue a teaching career. Data were gathered from the initial applications, from an evaluation survey administered on the last day of the Academy and from the reflections of a higher education visitor/observer from the University of Hawaii. The data suggest three major conclusions:

1. Attendees appear to be more definitive about why teaching would be self-fulfilling.
2. Attendees are aware of the complexities of pre-teaching preparation, the role of the teacher, and the importance of dedication and passion in teaching.
3. The selection of program content and invited speakers met the needs of the attendees.

To create broad-based support across the state of Ohio, the CAPE steering committee encourages local efforts to develop financial sponsors for CAPE participants. Local support can ensure the success of this special program in attracting talented young people of all backgrounds into the teaching profession. Founding sponsors include the Ohio Department of Education, Martha Holden Jennings Foundation, Ohio Minority Recruitment Consortium, Phi Delta Kappa International, Ohio Board of Regents, Teaching Leadership Consortium of Ohio, Ohio School Counselor Association, Ohio Association of Elementary School Administrators, and Ohio Association of Secondary School Administrators.

Testimonials from past CAPE participants:

"The teachers that show such enthusiasm and passion for what they do have convinced me that teaching is definitely the job for me, and I know that my passion for children will change lives thanks to CAPE."

"Listening to people talk about their calling to teaching and activities at other schools was really cool. The friendships are what made the experience exceptional."

"CAPE made me realize that I very much want to take on the challenges of being a teacher. Thanks for giving me the opportunity to come."

Universities play a major role in partnering with local school districts to bring life to the realm of the teaching profession. Below is a historical perspective of how Ashland University collaborated with interested parties to successfully recruit and retain future teachers for the profession.

Grow Your Own Initiatives in Ohio (Ashland University)

Background of the Development of Diversity Programs for the College of Education

During the early part of the 1989–90 Ashland University academic year, the dean of the College of Education appointed the director of the Bachelor's Plus Teacher Preparation Programs (Post Baccalaureate Graduate Program for the Ashland University system) to serve as a member of a group of Ohio educators regarding the establishment of a pre-collegiate minority teacher recruitment program for the state of Ohio. The Ohio Department of Education and numerous education organizations and individuals from across Ohio established the Camp Attracting Prospective Educators (CAPE). The CAPE program created a steering committee which was charged with developing a five-day summer residential teacher camp to be held at an Ohio college or university. A concerted effort would be made to attract students of color/underrepresented students into the teaching profession. The CAPE participants would be rising juniors and seniors from high schools throughout the state of Ohio. The program would accept up to 50 plus students per summer teacher camp.

Ashland University applied to the CAPE steering committee to host the first CAPE summer camp in Ohio. Ashland University was selected to host the first CAPE on its campus during the summer of 1992. The CAPE program became one of the cornerstones of the Ashland University College of Education Diversity programs as well as Ohio's minority teacher recruitment programs—particularly Grow Your Own programs. The CAPE program has been very successful and was offered again at an Ohio college or university during the summer of 2009 (number 17). Ashland University plans to apply to host the CAPE program on its campus during the summer of 2011. Another Ohio college will be hosting during the summers of 2009 and 2010.

During the early and mid-1990s, the Ashland University College of Education dean began educating faculty and administrators to the dynamics and escalating diversity of the K–12 student population in thousands of schools across the United States. The United States was becoming more racially, ethnically, and linguistically diverse than ever. This trend was expected to continue well into the twenty-first century. The reasons for this trend were higher birth rates among minority groups, particularly among African-Americans and Latinos; the differing age structure of each group which would contribute to higher fertility rates and lower death rates among persons of color, thereby increasing their share of the total population; and the net immigration was expected to be much higher for non-white groups in the decades to come. Combined, these factors would continue to transform the composition of the U.S. population over the next 45 years.

According to the U.S. Department of Commerce (1996), there were about 56.2 million five- to nineteen-year-olds in America. At that time, children of color constituted about one-third of the student population. Children of color were expected to become the numerical majority by 2035. By 2050, students of color would collectively account for about 57 percent of the student population in America.

Another important factor in the changing student population was the increasing numbers of limited-English-proficient students (LEP). The number of students in our schools who are English language learners has been growing at an average annual rate five times that of the total enrollment for over a decade. While advances have been made during that time to promote the effective education of ELLs, the body of teachers most qualified to accommodate their needs has been unable to match their growth (National Clearing House for Bilingual Education, 2001, p. 137).

Equally important was the increase in the number of students who are poor. Although the numerical majority of poor children in the United States were white, poverty was far more pervasive among racial and ethnic minority groups. Thus, as the numbers of students of racial/ethnic and linguistic minority grow in the years ahead, the poverty rate within the student population is likely to rise.

During the years to come, the problems associated with the achievement gaps between the white students and the black and Hispanic students would continue to be problematic and most likely would worsen. Those disparities would have to be addressed to ensure that all students would have access to educational and economic attainment. The primary source for this information is the book *Educating Culturally Responsive Teachers—A Coherent Approach*, by Anna Maria Villegas and Tamara Lucas, 2002.

Studies projected that, during the first decade of the twenty-first century, about 9 percent of teachers would be teachers of color (National Center for Educational Statistics, 1997). Students of color in schools at the national level were about 33 percent. In Ohio, about 20.76 percent of the students were projected to be students of color (National Center for Educational Statistics, 1997), while about 8 percent of Ohio's teachers were projected to represent minority groups (Ohio Department of Education, 1997).

But, who will teach them? A teacher shortage, combined with the necessary increase in STEM education, presents double trouble. African American, Latino and Native American teachers are already in short supply, not to mention the low number of whom are appropriately prepared to teach math and science (see http://www.teachers of color.com/2009/11).

During the 1970s through 1990s, the percentage of teachers of color in America's classrooms steadily declined. The demographics of the K–12 teachers in the United States contrasted dramatically with the student population in terms of race, culture, social class, and language.

In order to improve the educational programs and success for all students, more students of color had to be recruited into college teacher preparation programs, and into America's classrooms, and into Ohio classrooms. The universities had to prepare all of the teachers to be culturally responsive teachers.

During the early 1990s, the Ohio Department of Education made available to interested Ohio colleges and universities opportunities to apply for funds to develop Grow Your Own programs for recruitment of students ofcolor into the teaching profession by forming partnerships with selected public school districts. Ashland University College of Education applied for one of the grants. Ashland was awarded a grant to work with eight public school districts in north central, northern, and northeastern Ohio. The districts were Elyria City, Fremont City, Lorain City, Madison Local, Mansfield City, Oberlin City, Sandusky City, and Wooster City. Six of the districts were urban (Elyria, Fremont, Lorain, Mansfield, Oberlin, and Sandusky) with large African-American populations and many whites from the Appalachian Mountains area, with many of these students living in poverty. Elyria, Fremont, and Lorain also had large Latino populations, with many being impoverished. These urban districts also had many persons of European and Middle Eastern identities and ethnicities. Madison Local had a mixture of rural, growing African-American population, and a strong Appalachian culture. Wooster City had a large middle class, small but active African-American population, and a small number of European ethnicities. All eight districts had large numbers of Title I students, and most had older, rustbelt type heavy industries. Wooster had some modern industrial plants and businesses. All districts were subject to tough financial problems regarding support of their schools and failed levy and bond issues. However, all wanted more diversified teaching workforces with more teachers and administrators of color.

The Ashland University Grow Your Own grants (over four years) were used to establish and develop future Educator of America (FEA) chapters in each middle school, junior high school, and high school in each school district—a total of 23 schools with which Ashland University worked to develop interest among students to finish high school, attend a college/university, and consider teaching as a career. Each school district would work to recruit their own students back to their respective districts as teachers, thus Grow Your Own programs. The goals included the hiring of more teachers of color, male teachers for elementary classrooms, more female teachers for math and science areas, more teachers from the populations with disabilities, and more students from urban and rural backgrounds.

Ashland University's undergraduate Admission Office and the Bachelor's Plus program formed a university partnership to recruit traditional public school graduates and nontraditional adults with college degrees to enter the teacher preparation programs offered at Ashland University and its off-site centers in Lorain, Massillon, and Columbus. The university made arrangements to bring students form the 23 schools to Ashland for campus visits and tours, interaction with college students and professors from different academic disciplines and content areas. Students from the teacher preparation programs talked to the visiting students about college life and what it took to be successful in college, and why they chose to be teachers. The Admission Office staff talked about financial aid and scholarships available for students. Sending schools were also encouraged to bring parents of their students to Ashland so parents could learn about university programs and financial help for their children.

Ashland University also offered training and leadership workshops for teachers in the participating schools who were serving as advisors to their building FEA chapters. At the end of each school year, school FEA chapters would come to Ashland to participate in a regional FEA conference held in Ashland, Ohio, at the university.

Ashland also developed a "Public School Advisory Committee" from the eight school districts to advise and help promote and develop FEA chapters in these schools for service and help in their respective schools. The committee came to Ashland University in December of each year for a working luncheon meeting to continue forging the positive collaborative relationship which served teacher candidates.

The Ashland University Bachelor's Plus program set up an advisory committee in each school district to help find/recruit adults from their communities who wanted to be teachers. These adults would be sent back to the sending schools to do some field experience work and/or student teaching in their schools. Then they could hire their qualified adults back in their district schools—a Grow Your Own program.

The College of Education Diversity Committee was formed in the early 1990s and continues the work today to help the Grow Your Own school districts find applicants for teaching positions open in Ashland's College of Education. A Summer Dissertation Writing Fellowship was created to provide social and professional support to doctoral students from historically underrepresented groups in the writing of their dissertations. After these students completed their doctoral degrees, they were encouraged to apply and interview for teaching positions in the undergraduate and graduate teacher preparation programs.

What happened after Grow Your Own program grants? Ashland University actively participates in the Ohio Minority Recruitment Consortium as a member (since 1989). The major goal of this organization is to work on increasing diversity of Ohio's teaching force. Ohio Minority Recruitment Consortium was discussed earlier in this writing.

Ashland University Admission Office and Bachelor's Plus officials continue to connect with high schools and middle schools and discuss financial aid and formulas and other issues of student interest. The history of diversity efforts has provided a solid foundation to catapult the efforts to new levels. Today, Ashland University is maintaining these programs while avidly working on new initiatives to ensure diversity is seamless throughout the university and in the communities and on state, national, and international levels.

For example, Ashland University maintains an active role in the Council Attracting Prospective Educators (CAPE) program where the recruitment and retention of diversified students and teachers remains in the forefront on the agenda. A full-time Ashland University professor has co-chaired this program for the state of Ohio for two years. Plans are currently in the works for Ashland University hosting the CAPE Academy in 2011. A grant has been submitted to further these efforts and the connection with CAPE Academies scheduled throughout the state of Ohio. The CAPE program academy experiences are designed to attract talented young people from diverse backgrounds to an educational or teaching career.

A further step in increasing student diversity in which Ashland University is participating is the 2+2 program—a partnership with the Columbus State Community College where students entering their junior year come to Ashland University to take undergraduate courses (field work, study, teaching completed in area schools such as Columbus). Undergraduate recruiting for diversity is the focus at the Ashland University/Columbus Center.

During early 2009, the College of Education (COE) dean invited the vice president of Programs at the Cleveland Scholarship Programs (http://www.cspohio.org) to campus. During the meeting, which included the deans, financial aid, admissions, and others, a description of the program was presented; and it was decided that Ashland would be a viable site for the scholarships. In the past, a limited number of students had attended the University with the support of the program.

The provost offered scholarships to international undergraduate and graduate students whose high schools agree to partner with the institution as internship sites. Under this agreement, with the American School of Belo Horizonte, Brazil, Ashland will begin sending candidates to complete their internships in Brazil; and Ashland will offer academic scholarships to applicants from the American School of Belo Horizonte. This recruitment strategy is sustainable and replicable; it has a high likelihood of increasing the number of diverse candidates.

The University's strategic plan calls for the recruitment and retention of a diverse and academically strong student body that will benefit from the learning experiences provided. Another goal is internationalization—promoting the understanding of people and global issues—and provides experiences to prepare students to value other cultures, traditions, and languages to fulfill their global responsibilities.

The information provided here shows how a university is involved in the ultimate goal of recruitment and retention of diverse students to major in education for purposes of providing effective teachers for our classrooms of the future.*

The BECOME Program

The BECOME Program features a unique aspect of "Growing Your Own Teachers with business and education. This program is an exciting addition to harnessing the minority teacher prospects already in the pipeline. Details on how to set this program in to motion are provided below.

The BECOME (Business Education Collaboration on Minorities) Program was initiated by Fred L. Gissendaner, former personnel director, and Rosemary Endress, former counselor, Akron, Ohio Public Schools

The BECOME Program is another initiative to promote hiring minority teachers and is a pipeline program for Growing Your Own teachers featuring a partnership with business and education. This business education collaboration for minorities in education features an urban district working with a university and area businesses and organizations to support the diversity efforts of the district. The program supports quality minority educators specifically African-Americans, who have the desire to teach in Akron Public Schools.

Information is summarized here to give the reader specific, detailed information for possible inclusion in a district setting. The idea/origin of the idea, thought processes, data need, connections, resources, and impact are all addressed here for purposes of providing another avenue to secure effective, qualified teachers for the future.

---

*For information on Ashland University's Grow Your Own initiatives, please contact Dr. Janet E. Kearney-Gissendaner: jkearney@ashland.edu

During the summer of 1990, Rosemary Endress, counselor at Central-Hower High School, discussed the need to increase the minority teaching staff by offering opportunities for promising young students to become teachers. In November 1990, Ms. Endress and Mr. Gissendaner, personnel director, completed and submitted to the assistant superintendent of Personnel Services of the Akron Public Schools a proposal outlining a program to increase minority teachers.

In January of 1991, Dr. Trenta, executive director, wrote to Jack Heckel, president and chief operating officer of GenCorp, relaying to him the findings of a report of the Akron Public School's Study Committee on the Akron 2000 goals. One of the reports addressed the concerns of the lack of minorities teaching in the Akron Public Schools.

In the year of 1991, nearly 41 percent of enrolled students in Akron Public Schools were minority students. In that same year, only 14 percent of the teaching force was minority. The report recommended "the hiring of more minority teachers and administrators." The report further stated, "Because there is a need for a more culturally diverse staff, the Akron Board of Education and Administration should devise and institute a more pro-active and aggressive recruitment and hiring plan with finite goals and timetables that will effectively address the under-representation of minorities, especially African-Americans, in the professional classifications. The administration should develop and implement a systemwide, comprehensive culturally diverse training program as soon as possible."

"Minority students," the report continued, "especially African-Americans, need positive role models. Further, our teachers must have a better understanding of and be more sensitive to cultural differences." A position paper was developed by the Ohio Minority Recruitment Consortium, a standing committee of the Ohio Association of School Personnel Administrators, of which Mr. Gissendaner was a member. This paper outlined several reasons for increasing the number of minority teachers and outlined a recruitment strategy. The following steps were taken by Mr. Gissendaner to increase the number of minorities in the classrooms:

1. Re-establish contact with Southern college campuses and visit over twenty.

2. Participate in Kent State University Job Fair, Teach Ohio Job Fair in Columbus, Central State Career Day, Expo-Ohio Northern University, Cleveland State Teacher Fair.
3. Develop a Minority Recruitment Day.
4. Participate in a seminar titled "Developing Local Teacher Talent: Encouraging Minority Students to Pursue Careers in Education."
5. Purchase an ad in the *Black Collegian*, the national magazine for Black college students with a circulation of over 100,000).

More needed to be done, however. Additional steps needed to be taken within the community, at the high school level, to recruit minority educators. A funding proposal was created by Mr. Gissendaner and Ms. Endress and sent to GenCorp (community resource).

Additional steps were taken within the community at the high school level to recruit minority educators. The proposed program was outlined to GenCorp and included the following initial steps:

1. Initiate a sales pitch to all high school counselors working with the classes of 1991 and 1993.
2. Distribute brochures and applications to all counselors.
3. Conduct an invitation-only presentation for minority students with a 2.5 cumulative GPA in a high school auditorium.
4. Offer applications to all minority students who are interested and meet the criteria established.
5. Screen applications with an appointed committee.

The proposal further suggested that students entering the "unnamed program" would sign a contract which would guarantee paid tuition and possibly room and board at cooperating colleges and universities. Once the student completed schooling they would have opportunity to have their school loan forgiven by teaching in Akron. Akron Public Schools would hire all qualified applicants, providing there was a need for their discipline. Curricular counseling would occur while the student was in school to determine which disciplines were needed upon graduation. After four years of teaching in Akron Public Schools, the loan would be forgiven. The original proposal included provisions for minority students to attend the college or university of their choice nationwide, receive corporate sponsored summer employment from Akron Public Schools for each summer of their academic career, and have a minority teacher as a mentor throughout the program.

The proposal was submitted to GenCorp, a company interested in supporting education issues in the community. The proposal was accepted with modifications. This was the beginning of the BECOME (Business Education Collaboration on Minorities in Education Program, under the direction of an administrator. GenCorp agreed to provide $1000 per year for four or five years for five select students. GenCorp's original proposal from the fall of 1991 specified several qualifications for scholarship recipients. High school students must:

- ◆ Have high school senior status and be enrolled in a college preparatory course of study.
- ◆ Have obtained a minimum SAT combined score of 800, or an ACT score of 18.
- ◆ Have a minimum 2.75 grade-point average.
- ◆ Have applied to Kent State University or The University of Akron.
- ◆ Have interest in pursuing a degree necessary for teaching.

Post-secondary students were also to be considered for the program. They must:

- ◆ Be at least a second-year student at the University of Akron or Kent State.
- ◆ Have a minimum of 2.5 grade-point average.
- ◆ Be interested in a career in education.

College graduates would be considered if they:

- ◆ Completed a four-year college degree program.
- ◆ Were interested in retraining as educators.

Manager of INROADS Northeast Ohio was named as an advisor. Guidelines were established for the program. Grade-point average was established, qualifications, details of student selection, and the interviewing process was confirmed.

A planning committee was selected after GenCorp committed to the program plan. Members represented a cross section of organizations: business, public schools, higher education. High school seniors and education majors were recruited from the University of Akron and Kent State University.

Finances for the BECOME program were derived from scholarships from the University of Akron or Kent State University and a forgivable loan from a donating corporation. The final agreement included a $500 scholarship from each University and local businesses (only GenCorp in the first year) matching each scholarship with a $1,000 forgivable loan. The package was in force for five years. Students who were offered teaching jobs would have twenty-five percent of their debt forgiven for each year spent teaching in Akron Public Schools.

BECOME provided offers of summer jobs to the participants. For the first two summers (pre-college and post-freshman year), the sponsoring company would be responsible for providing summer employment. The summer job during year three was provided by the sponsoring university and in year four the student would be employed by Akron Public Schools.

College graduates were considered if they had a four-year college degree program and were interested in retraining as educators. Guidelines were established for the program, such as grade-point average, how and where to recruit students, establishment of the interviewing process, and other details.

Financial backing was committed from GenCorp Company, Equal Opportunity and Affirmative Action, and a planning committee was selected. Members represented a wide variety of professions: INROADS Northeast Ohio; College of Education, Akron University; Akron High School; Equal Opportunity & Affirmative Action, GenCorp; Director of Professional Employment and Certification, Akron Public Schools; Coordinator of Community Partnerships, Akron Public Schools; Coordinator Recruitment/Student Life, Kent State University; Executive Director of Community/Adult Partnerships, Akron Public Schools; Assistant Dean for Student Life, Kent State University; Vice President of Communications, GenCorp.

College graduates were considered based on the following criteria:

◆ Have completed a four-year college degree program.
◆ Are interested in retraining as educators.

The BECOME Program is a program that could easily be set up in school districts across the nation to "grow" prospective teachers in the pipeline. For information to start-up a similar program, contact 330-761-2818

South Carolina State Teachers Cadet Program—History and Goal

Center for Educator Recruitment, Retention and Advancement, Rock Hill, SC
Contact: 803-323-4032, Ext. 6408, or 800-476-2387.

"We cannot adequately prepare the coming generation if the least able students enter the profession. Teaching must become a top priority and gifted students must be recruited."—Dr. Ernest Boyer

A Brief History

South Carolina's Teacher Cadet Program can trace its origins to a small but innovative program at Conway High School in the Horry County School District. In the late 1970s, foreign language teacher Bonner Guidera began using part of her planning period to work with a few of Conway High's outstanding students. The students—all of whom had an interest in learning more about the art and craft of teaching—were given opportunities to tutor high school students and to work as aides in the elementary schools.

In 1984, Ms. Guidera and two fellow teachers decided to seek a grant from the Carnegie Foundation for the Advancement of Teaching to expand their informal effort into a structured course available to high-achieving students. The teachers submitted a grant application for a "Cadet Teacher" program, using a description from the literature of the Carnegie Foundation for the Advancement of Teaching, which drew from Carnegie president Ernest Boyer's 1983 book, *High School: A Report on Secondary Education in America.*

Although the Conway grant proposal was not funded by Carnegie, the idea of a Cadet course attracted the attention of Dr. Jim Rex, then dean of the Winthrop College (S.C.) School of Education. Using a special appropriation, Winthrop had established a teacher recruitment task force in 1984 made up of representatives from most of the state's colleges and education associations. The task force was looking for worthy projects to further its goals and began to explore the Cadet idea under the leadership of Dr. Patricia Graham, Winthrop's director of special projects.

With a promise of grant support from Winthrop, four high schools agreed to serve as pilot sites for the Cadet program during the 1985–86 school year. The schools also agreed to form partnerships with nearby colleges and to involve college faculty in the teaching of an introduction to education course.

As the Cadet pilot programs were getting underway in the fall of 1985, the Educator Recruitment Task Force organized by Winthrop was in the midst of preparing a grant application for $236,000 in state funds earmarked for teacher recruitment. The Task Force, which now represents all 28 colleges in South Carolina offering teacher education, was awarded the grant by the state Commission on Higher Education and moved at once to establish the S. C. Center for Teacher Recruitment. Today, the Center receives annual state appropriations for all its recruitment work, including the Teacher Cadet Program.

Steady Growth

During the spring of 1986, the Center initiated plans to expand the Teacher Cadet network. High school principals from each of the state's more than 200 high schools were invited to attend a meeting to discuss the Cadet concept. By 1988–90, 101 high schools were offering the Teacher Cadet Program serving over fourteen hundred students and partnering with nineteen colleges.

Five years later, during the 1994–95 school year, enrollment grew to over 2,200 students. The Teacher Cadet Program was being offered at 141 high schools partnered with 24 colleges.

Further expansion has brought the number of high schools offering Teacher Cadet during the 1997–98 year to 147 with 23 partner colleges and universities teaching an average of 2,600 students each year.

Several schools have experienced such demand for the course that they offer two sections of the program. Approximately one-fourth of the Cadets are male, and over one-third are minority students.

Program Goals

The Teacher Cadet Program is considered an introduction or orientation to the teaching profession. Its main purpose is to encourage students who possess a high level of academic achievement and the personality traits found in good teachers to consider teaching as a career. Although the course is taught at a college freshman level, the curriculum includes simulations and other "hands-on" activities designed to excite students about teaching.

Students are exposed to teaching careers and the education system through class discussions, observation and participation in public school classrooms, and interactions with successful administrators and teachers. An important secondary goal of the program is to provide these talented future community leaders with insights about schools.

Criteria for Participation

The Center provides site grants to each school to help support the program. This grant provides support for the class, for teacher training and materials, and for college involvement. Schools may enter into a partnership with a college, or they may choose to operate independently. Independent sites receive financial support for speakers.

In return for the grant support and the support of the Center staff during the year, high schools and colleges agree to meet reasonable criteria set by the Center. All students enrolled in the program must have a grade point ration (GPR) of at least 3.0 on a 4-point scale (or be recommended by a TC review panel for those eligible applicants with a GPR very close to approaching 3.0), must be enrolled in college prep courses, and must be recommended by five teachers. Recommended class size is 15 students.

Program Evaluation

The Teacher Cadet Program has attracted state and national attention. In November 1988, the task force studying the future of education improvement in South Carolina recommended the program be expanded to all school districts in South Carolina. School systems in Washington, California, Tennessee, Oklahoma, Georgia, Arkansas, Maryland, Michigan, Mississippi, New York, North Carolina, Massachusetts, Virginia, Nevada, Louisiana, and Texas have implemented the SC Teacher Cadet model; other states have expressed interest in the program.

An external evaluation is completed annually of the Teacher Cadet Program. Am impressive average of 38% of all students who have taken part in the TC program indicate they plan to teach. The average SAT score for Cadets has consistently been about 100 points higher than the average SC student and 50 points higher than the national average. A study done by the University of South Carolina Educational Policy Center in Georgia and North and South Carolina found that only 4% of a sample of high-achieving non-Cadet high school students planned to enter teaching. Over 2,500 former Cadets are currently teaching in SC. Fifteen percent of these teachers indicated at the end of the TCP that they did not want to teach but, in fact, did change to teaching as a career choice while in college.

The Teacher Cadet Program was selected by CBS for inclusion in a two-hour prime time documentary on American education in 1990. More recently, the Teacher Cadet Program was also featured in articles in both *Educational Leadership* and *Kappan* and has been referred to as "a national prototype" for pre-collegiate teacher recruitment programs.

Teacher Cadet Curriculum Components

Participants in the South Carolina Teacher Cadet network are expected to include certain fundamental components in their Teacher Cadet courses, whether taught for high school credit or college credit, with or without a college partner.

The components of the Teacher Cadet course are intentionally broad in scope and provide a great deal of flexibility to the high school and college teacher. Where college credit is being offered, teachers should have no difficulty matching most of these elements to existing curriculum and adapting where necessary. We continue to stress that the Teacher Cadet curriculum should not be a "foundations" course. It is an introduction to teaching and education that must include field experiences.

Teacher Cadet Curriculum Components

The Learner
◆ Self-assessment
◆ The role of self-esteem
◆ Exploration of personal values, beliefs, and attitudes
◆ Personality styles and learning styles
◆ Personal, intellectual, linguistic, and social human growth and development
◆ Observations of students at various development stages
◆ Appreciating diversity and multiculturalism
◆ Special needs students
◆ Barriers to learning

The School
◆ The history of schools
◆ Adapting and changing
◆ Curriculum trends
◆ The governance of schools (state and local)
◆ Society's expectations of schools
◆ Roles of school personnel (district and school building level)

- ◆ The school curriculum (state requirements, philosophical issues)
- ◆ Organization and management of schools (district staff presentations)
- ◆ school reform movement (state and national)
- ◆ Current issues facing schools
- ◆ Different kinds of schools

The Teacher and Teaching
- ◆ Characteristics of today's teachers
- ◆ Teacher responsibilities
- ◆ Attitudes of teachers
- ◆ Multiple intelligences
- ◆ Learning modalities
- ◆ Exploring instructional models
- ◆ Classroom culture
- ◆ Discipline and management
- ◆ Exploring careers in education
- ◆ Teacher supply and demand issues
- ◆ Intrinsic and extrinsic benefits of teaching
- ◆ Field experience with a classroom teacher
- ◆ SAY (Science and Youth)
- ◆ MAY (Math and Youth)
- ◆ FLAY (Foreign Language and Youth)
- ◆ Portfolios
- ◆ Teacher Cadet Closing Ceremonies

Field Experience

In addition to the fundamental curriculum components, all students are required to observe and participate in classrooms at the primary/elementary, middle/junior high, and secondary levels. Provisions should also be made for Cadets to observe and to participate in a variety of settings, including special education classes, pre-school children programs (e.g., public school programs for four-year olds, day care centers and nursery schools), remedial/compensatory programs and vocational/technical programs.

- ◆ *Observations*. Students will observe in classrooms throughout the year based on the content of the curriculum. For example, after studying human growth and development characteristics of children ages 6 through 12, Cadets will observe students of that age in a public school classroom. Observations should be structured and should be based on specific objectives. Prior to these observations, students should be trained in observation skills (e.g., collecting data, making inferences, and drawing conclusions).
- ◆ *Extended Field Experience*. The extended field experience typically occurs in early spring in a traditional year-long class, during which time the students are placed in a classroom under the supervision of a master teacher. (The timing of the extended field experience for Teacher Cadets on an A/B or 4x4 schedule should be adjusted to occur fairly late in the course and allow adequate time for the Cadets to get a complete experience, including bonding with the younger students. This is the magical part of the Teacher Cadet experience—the hook that will grab potential teachers—and it should be utilized effectively.) The Teacher Cadets may be placed at the elementary, middle, or high school level, depending on their content interests. Cadets should continue to attend their TCP class at least one day each week during the extended field experience in order to plan and process their experiences.

    Types of teaching and observing experiences may include, but are not limited to, the following: peer tutoring; tutoring; serving as an assistant to a master teacher; planning and teaching lessons to a small or large group of students; planning and developing learning centers; and serving as a laboratory assistant.

Teacher Cadet Program—Core Curriculum Standards

Teacher Cadets will:

Standard 1:   Understand themselves as individuals, learners, and community members.

Standard 2:   Demonstrate respect for themselves and the diversity of those they will teach.

Standard 3:   Examine the physical, cognitive, moral, and psychosocial developmental characteristics of learners from birth through adulthood.

Standard 4:   Identify and evaluate teaching strategies that will benefit learners with special needs.

Standard 5:   Analyze the effects of challenges faced by learners from diverse backgrounds.

Standard 6:   Understand historical and current educational issues, policies, and practices.

Standard 7:   Comprehend how schools are governed at the local, state, and national levels.

Standard 8:   Examine the roles of the teacher within the profession.

Standard 9:   Demonstrate various methods to deliver lessons creatively and effectively.

Standard 10:   Apply their knowledge by observing, assisting, and teaching in a classroom.

The State of Ohio Initiatives

There have been significant state initiatives to assist Ohio school districts with recruiting a more diverse teacher workforce.

These programs are briefly described as follows:

Ohio Core Initiatives

♦ The state has funded Ohio Core Initiatives to help districts with providing their high-need schools with high quality teachers. Currently, the state has developed and funded partnerships with colleges and universities to train already licensed teachers to become certified in high-need subjects. This is a 12-month intensive training program for licensed teachers in Ohio and mid-career professionals to teach science, math, or foreign language, which are three of the state's subject area shortages. Funding for this program is three years, starting in FY-07–FY-09.

♦ In FY 09, the state budget funded two new programs to provide incentives for foreign language, science, and mathematics teachers to teach in hard-to-staff schools. The signing bonus program is funded at $4.0 million, and the loan forgiveness program is funded at $2.5 million. To qualify for either program, an individual must be licensed, assigned to teach in foreign language, science, or mathematics, and agree to teach in a hard-to-staff traditional public school for a minimum of five years. An individual who has met all requirements will receive either a $20,000 signing bonus or $20,000 in loan forgiveness.

State Transition to Teaching Grant (OSU and ODE State Partnership Grant-this program is no longer funded at this time)

♦ In 2002, Ohio was awarded a Transition to Teaching grant from the U.S. Department of Education. The five-year grant was to recruit, train, and support alternatively licensed teachers. Fifty (50) candidates were selected each year, for a total of 250 candidates. These candidates taught in high-need districts and received mentoring support, online tutorial preparation for the Principles of Learning and Teaching (PLT) assessment, and guidance in completing requirements to acquire their two-year provisional license.

TEACH Ohio Grants

♦ State funds supported a partnership with participating colleges and universities to recruit, train, and support qualifying candidates to teach in subject area shortages like science and math in Ohio high-need school districts. Candidates matriculated through a graduate-level program earning credits leading towards a master's degree and received mentoring support at school and at the university.

Technical Assistance to School Districts

◆ The Office of Educator Equity (OEE) provided technical assistance to school districts by conducting a presentation on national efforts to recruit and retain minority teachers in high-need school districts at the Ohio Minority Recruitment Consortium (OMRC) on September 26, 2007. OMRC requested OEE to share information on this topic.

Alternative Paths to Teacher Licensure Requirements

◆ The Center for the Teaching Profession is committed to the recruitment and retention of high-quality teachers and principals, expanding the pool of capable teachers and principals and making it easier for Ohio schools to hire and retain good teachers.

Conditional and alternative paths to teacher licensure permit qualified baccalaureate degree-holders to transition to careers as classroom teachers. Information and resources related to Ohio's conditional/alternative licensure programs, for content area teachers, grades 7–12 follows.

◆ **Requirements for a Conditional Teaching Permit (for Grades 7–12)**
  ◆ Baccalaureate degree.
  ◆ Background check via BCII and FBI (for out-of-state applicants).
  ◆ Applicant must pass the basic skills test prescribed by the State Board of Education.

- Applicants are required to have the Educational Testing Service send the Praxis I score report directly to the Office of Certification/Licensure. Photocopies of Praxis I score reports are not acceptable. Ohio's recipient number is R7945.
- Applicant must complete 15 semester hours (or equivalent) in the teaching area of subject area for which license is sought, either as part of the applicant's degree program or in addition to the baccalaureate degree.
- Applicant must complete six semester hours (or equivalent) of additional coursework in previous five years, with a minimum GPA of 2.5 (out of 4.0); coursework must be acceptable to applicant's prospective employer and must be in one or more of the following areas: teaching content area, characteristics of student learning, diversity of learners, planning instruction, instructional strategies, learning environments, communication, assessment, and/or student support; coursework may be provided by regional professional development providers if taken for credit in collaboration with a college or university that is approved by the State Board of Education to provide teacher education.
- Permit (one-year non-renewable) is issued at request of superintendent of employing school district.
- Prospective employing school district agrees to provide a structured mentoring program.
- Applicant agrees to complete an additional three semester hours of coursework in teaching or content area, while employed under the conditional permit.
- Applicant agrees to seek an Alternative Educator License at the end of the year for which the Conditional Teaching Permit is issued.
- **Requirements for an Alternative Education License (for Grades 7–12)**
  - Provide evidence of the additional three semester hours of coursework in teaching or content area,

completed while employed under the conditional permit (for those entering through the Conditional Permit route).

- ◆ Applicant must hold baccalaureate degree with a GPA of 2.5 or higher in major (the content area to be taught) or extensive work experience directly related to the content area.
- ◆ Applicant must pass prescribed content area examination (Praxis II content area test).
- ◆ Applicant must complete six semester hours (or the equivalent) of professional education coursework within the past five years with a GPA of 2.5, and from a college or university approved to prepare teachers, as follows: three hours in teaching methods, including field experience, and three hours in developmental characteristics of adolescent youths.
- ◆ License (two-year non-renewable) is issued on verification of employment by superintendent of school district; employing school district agrees to provide a structured mentoring program.

◆ **Requirements for a Provisional Educator License**
  - ◆ Applicant must complete two years of teaching under the alternative license.
  - ◆ Applicant must successfully complete (with a GPA of 2.5 or higher) at least 12 additional semester hours (or the equivalent) of college coursework in the principles and practices of teaching, student development and learning, pupil assessment procedures, curriculum development, classroom management, and teaching methodology.
  - ◆ Applicant must pass the appropriate assessment of professional knowledge (Praxis II test in the principles of learning and teaching).

◆ **Requirements for a Professional Educator License**
  - ◆ Applicant must complete a structured mentoring program, provided by employing school district that is congruent with the performance assessment required for entry year teachers.

♦ Applicant must pass performance-based assessment by state-appointed evaluator (Praxis III); license is renewed every five years, pending completion of prescribed professional development activities.

Contact Information
Office of Educator Licensure
Email: Educator.Licensure@ode.state.oh.us
Phone (614) 466-3593.

Troops to Teachers

Troops to Teachers, or TTT, was established in 1994 to help recruit quality teachers that serve students in high-need schools throughout America. TTT helps relieve teacher shortages, especially in math, science, special education, and other critical subject areas, and assists military personnel in making successful transitions to second careers in teaching. The goal of this legislation was to help improve American education by providing motivated, experienced, and dedicated personnel for the nation's classrooms. The three main objectives of the program were:

1. Help relieve teacher shortages.
2. Provide positive role models for the nation's public school students.
3. Assist military personnel to successfully transition to teaching as a second career. Federal funding may be provided to eligible individuals as stipends up to $5,000 to help pay for teacher certification costs or as bonuses of $10,000 to teach in a high-need school.

The Troops to Teachers Program is not a certification/licensing program. For example, to teach in Ohio, you must be licensed by the Ohio Department of Education. Two options to enter the classroom are by completing a traditional teacher education program or meet the requirements through a non-traditional route via Ohio's Alternative Educator License.

Troops to Teachers Contact Information
Veronica Hampton
Email: Veronica.Hampton@ode.state.oh.us
Phone: (614) 466-4283 or 1-800-852-6064 toll free

Urban Teaching Academies

The rationale for Urban Teaching Academies (UTAs) is that, as a nation, we say that our goal is to leave no child behind; but the schools we provide for some children say otherwise. Low-performing urban schools typically have high concentrations of inexperienced teachers who are too often unprepared for the challenges they face. The teacher dropout rate is often higher than the student dropout rate.

These struggling schools rarely close the teaching quality gap, let alone the student achievement gap, because they are constantly rebuilding their staff. As teachers head for the exits, they cite poor preparation, insufficient classroom support, and inadequate opportunities for career advancement. To break this cycle, the National Commission on Teaching and America's Future (NCTAF) launched an Urban Teaching Academies initiative with the support of MetLife Foundation to provide quality teaching in high-priority schools. (See http://www.nctaf .org/resources/demonstration_projects/urban_teaching/ index.htm.)

Urban Teaching Academies (UTAs) develop and retain teachers who are well prepared to teach in urban settings through the melding of teacher preparation with practical clinical experience in urban classrooms. Drawing on many of the features of teaching hospital/medical residency programs, Teaching Academies build effective urban teaching teams of teacher candidates (often called "residents") who observe and work alongside veteran teachers in specially selected training schools (often called "teaching academies"). Residents integrate their daily classroom experiences with what they are learning from formal teacher education courses that are held on-site at their academy after school hours. The residents' academic coursework is sequenced around the teaching cycle of the school year and their content and methods courses are well aligned to the host school district curriculum standards and student learning needs. On-site preparation with guided practice and collaborative teamwork focused on improving teaching quality and student achievement in high-priority schools is at the heart of an Urban Teacher Academy.

In 2006, NCTAF and MetLife Foundation recognized and awarded grants to three Urban Teaching Academies. Why were these models selected? NCTAF identified three programs that have taken promising approaches to meeting the needs of urban schools through the teaching academy model. The goal of the NCTAF—MetLife Foundation grants is to put a national spotlight on these programs so that others might learn from them, and to help each program advance its goals. The three programs are:

◆ Academy for Urban School Leadership (AUSL), founded in 2001 as a nonprofit organization in Chicago, Illinois, is the first teacher training academy in the nation to partner directly with a school district to recruit, train, and place certified, highly-qualified, and well-educated teachers. Today, AUSL is supported through a unique public-private partnership; and each year recruits 45 to 60 mid-career professionals and recent college graduates to participate in an intensive 12-month clinical teacher preparation program. See http://www.ausl-chicago.org.

◆ California State University at Long Beach (CSULB) offers four specialized masters degree programs to cohorts of practicing teachers delivered entirely at their elementary schools at Long Beach. The content of these programs is tailored to the specific needs of the school, based on goals set forth in each site's School Effectiveness Plan. A pre-service residency program at these schools will be added to the CSULB program, with the graduates of the masters program serving as the mentor teachers.

◆ Montclair State University's Urban Teaching Academy (UTA) was created in 2001 and works with schools in urban Newark and Patterson, New Jersey. This program has three key elements: intensive and well-supervised school-based field experiences; community-based internships; and explicit attention to teacher candidates' notions regarding race, culture, and social justice. The program also has an early childhood cohort recruited exclusively from nearby Essex and Passaic County Community Colleges creating a seamless "Pipeline to Teaching" educational program leading to early childhood certification.

5

Prepare for Action

Stakeholder Responsibilities

Stakeholders must be a central focus of this process of recruitment and retention of minority teachers. Examine their responsibilities and begin to think about how you will incorporate some of these ideas and/or expound upon what you already have in operation. Policies are needed that recognize the changes to be made in the personnel management system for preparation of a district minority recruitment and retention plan. See Figure 5.1.

The School Personnel Management System (SPMS) is an excellent tool to begin an assessment of stakeholder responsibilities (Harrington-Leuker, 1996). Please refer to this reference for the details of responsibilities from school board members, superintendent, central office administrators, principals, and all administrators and staff.

Action Plan

Also in this chapter, you will find an action plan (Figure 5.2) to use in setting up a minority teacher recruitment and retention model. Examine this content and begin immediately in setting your goals and timelines. You may already have many components in operation—if so, just expound upon them. Or change them to meet your district's needs.

Minority/Diverse Teacher Recruitment Model Survey

A survey (Figure 5.3) follows with questions about your district to assist you in the process of planning your program. Recruitment strategies are listed to spark interest in areas that you have already explored, and others that might be added to boost your efforts. Exemplary characteristics of program models are provided to set standards that you will work toward. Revisit the exemplary models provided in this writing. Be creative!

The School Personnel Management System (SPMS) is an excellent tool to begin an assessment of stakeholder responsibilities (Harrington-Leuker, 1996). Please refer to this reference for the details of responsibilities from school board members, superintendent, central office administrators, principals, and all administrators and staff.

Your Challenge

Attracting and retaining highly effective teachers is a challenge according to Info Brief of the Association of Supervision and Curriculum Development (ASCD), which further describes lockstep teacher compensation systems that ensure uniformity and predictability for teachers and the school boards who pay for them (Rasmussen, 1999). But, you can make a change by taking action! I challenge you to:

1. Use multiple approaches.
2. Welcome minorities in your community and culture!
3. Realize the changing demographics.
4. Not wait on the school board to question why you are not hiring a certain number/percentage of teachers—show them! Track your hire data. Be pro-active.
5. Make it your responsibility to keep your superintendent informed; formulate policy. Work with your district's superintendent cabinet, policymakers within the district, advisory groups.

6. Make it a goal to obtain superintendent support and sign off on it.
7. Seek advocacy groups in community (NAACP, Urban League, Ministerial Alliance, sororities, fraternities, churches, and other groups that may help).

The key to a successful process is connection and collaboration of all parties involved. Uncover the strengths in your staff and place them into action with your plan!

FIGURE 5.1 Who Are the Stakeholders?

Boards/ Superintendents	◆ Lead in Policy development (i.e., board legislation: affirmative action, set goals, hiring, transfer policy)
Human Resource Officials	◆ Personnel Management ◆ Strategies for recruitment/ retention and operations
District Personnel Administrators	◆ Develop a minority teacher recruitment plan ◆ Lead in diversifying data, staff profiles; data management to determine focus and strategy
Principals	◆ Identify future teachers ◆ Pipeline program operation ◆ Mentor/Induction of Teachers ◆ Grow Your Own program ◆ Selection/assignments ◆ K–12 initiative Programs

FIGURE 5.1 Who Are the Stakeholders? *(continued)*

Principals *(continued)*	◆ Academies—Teacher/Partners
	  ◆ CAPE/CARE pipeline participation
	  ◆ Program participation
	  ◆ (FEA/FTA
	  ◆ Phi Delta Kappa)

Central Office Administrators	◆ Personnel Policies development ◆ School Personnel Management System (SPMS); data management
Curriculum/ Instruction Specialists/ Administrators/ Teachers	◆ Professional development connection program; mentoring ◆ Induction, programming
State Board of Education	◆ Grants ◆ Local board of education— policy ◆ Partnerships ◆ Teacher academies ◆ CAPE/CARE Programs; grants

FIGURE 5.2 Action plan

Minority (Diverse) Teacher Recruitment Model Plan/Program

Goal	Method/Strategy	Timeline	Person Responsible
1. Obtain data on teacher hires by race/gender % and MAs yearly			
2. Establish/Identify stakeholders and responsibilities—determine goals for minority teacher plan			
3. Devise a sample minority teacher recruitment plan to meet district needs			

FIGURE 5.2 Action plan *(continued)*

Goal	Method/Strategy	Timeline	Person Responsible
4. Build and implement Pipeline programs—school, university, state level—establish partnerships			
5. Evaluate and review research data yearly to determine changes/updates			
6. Seek funding (grants and other sources) for programming			

FIGURE 5.3
Source: AASPA

Minority/Diverse Teacher Recruitment Model Survey

The following model is provided for all organizations to complete with their unique information regarding their status of minority hires and other information utilitzed to build a successful program.

Directions:

Please complete the following questions about your district/ organization to provide important information on minority/ diverse recruitment model programs and/or district data.

Name: _____

Position: _____

Title: _____

District Name/Location: _____

District Type (Please Check):
_____ Urban _____ Suburban _____ Rural _____ Other

Total Hires for School Year: 2009–10 _____
Racial Composition:	No. %
1. Caucasian	_____
2. Black	_____
3. Hispanic	_____
4. Alaskan/Native American	_____
5. Asian/Pacific Islander	_____

Total Hires for School Year: 20__–20__ _____
Racial Composition:	No. %
1. Caucasian	_____
2. Black	_____
3. Hispanic	_____
4. Alaskan/Native American	_____
5. Asian/Pacific Islander	_____

FIGURE 5.3 *(continued)*

Review Annually

1. Do you have a minority (diverse) recruitment program in your district? Please describe and highlight your program and plan, or a plan you would like to have for your district.

2. Is your program successful (or what constitutes a successful plan)? Why, or why not? Describe why or why not.

3. How do you evaluate your success, or how would you evaluate success? (summative data)

4. How does, or how would, district/organizational culture affect your program? Describe what you do to make people welcome to the school, district, and community.

5. What are barriers to district efforts to attract and retain minority (diverse) teachers? Please describe.

6. Please define an exemplary minority/diverse teacher recruitment program. Describe in detail.

7. Please check the following strategies and related programs you utilize to enhance your minority (diverse) teacher recruitment program. Please describe (checked ones) each on the back of the sheet.

FIGURE 5.3 *(continued)*

Review Annually
Strategies

___ Special recruitment efforts at colleges and universities
___ Recruit at historically Black/Hispanic colleges
___ International recruitment efforts
___ Incentives (e.g., housing assistance, relocation benefits, financial, salary, etc.)
___ Waive certain job/licensure requirements
___ School placement guarantees
___ Offer on-the-spot contracts
___ Offer induction/support programs
___ Offer alternative certification routes
___ Offer monetary bonus for talented/high-need subject area candidates
___ Offer bonus for high student achievement
___ Offer loan forgiveness program
___ Tuition assistance for graduate course work
___ Incentives for NBPTS certification
___ City or county residency requirement
___ Provide guidance and information about teacher credentialing
___ Sponsor job fairs to attract new teachers to school district
___ Provide teacher employment information via telephone hotline
___ Participate in online counseling and/or job-finding services or website
___ Establish partnerships with teacher education programs
___ Streamline hiring process
___ Utilize alternative licensure procedures/assist out-of-state candidates
___ Establish searches for non-traditional teachers
___ Non-traditional programs, i.e., Troops to Teachers
___ Grow Your Own program for students in elementary/middle/high school
___ Retention strategies for minorities/diverse
___ Induction programs/teacher orientation
___ Teacher academy/professional development activities
___ Other

FIGURE 5.3 *(continued)*

Review Annually
Characteristics of Exemplary Minority Recruitment Programs
- ◆ High numbers and percentages of diverse staff
- ◆ High retention rate of minority
- ◆ Established networks: school/community/partnerships/universities/"Grow Your Own" programs/ minority consortiums/CAPE/Prospective teacher programs/regional networks support
- ◆ Support of district/aggressive recruitment plan/ budget to support/grants
- ◆ Quality teacher selection instruments (valid and reliable)
- ◆ Program development: such as, New Teacher Academy, Columbus Educators of Tomorrow, CAPE/CARE, FTA, FEA, Induction/Orientation programs, Mentor Programs
- ◆ Computerized bank of candidates

FIGURE 5.3 *(continued)*

Review Annually
Summary

In summary, briefly describe *outstanding* characteristics of your minority teacher recruitment program model. What is your district/organization minority teacher program emphasis, or what should be your district/organization minority teacher program emphasis?

Thank you for your time in completing this survey. Information provided will be useful for future direction for minority teacher recruitment models.

Recommended Resources

American School Board Journal
http://www.asbj.com

Center for Educator Retention, Recruitment, and Advancement
http://www.cerra.org/careers/altpathways

Education World Administrators Center: NEA Offers Tips
http://www.education-world.com/a_admin/admin171.shtml

List of Historically Black Colleges and Universities (HBCU).
http://en.wikipedia.org/wiki/Historically_black_colleges_
and_universities
http://www.hbcuconnect.com

Grant sites for minority teacher recruitment and retention
http://www.USAFundingApplications.org.

National School Board Assoication
http://www.nsba.org

Online Education
http://www.educationconnection.com

**Teacher Recruitment and Retention: Current Programs and
Legislation in the 109th Congress, University of North Texas**
http://digital.library.unt.edu/ark:/67531/metacrs5865/

The Alliance for Quality Teaching
http://www.qualityteaching.org

UNCF Member Colleges
http://www.uncf.org/members/index.asp

References

Berrigan, A. (RNT), & Schwartz, S. (CGCS). (2000). *Urban Teacher Academy Project Toolkit: A Guide to Developing High School Teaching Career Academies.* Available at http://www .eric.ed.gov/ERICDocs/data/ericdocs2sql/content_ storage_01/0000019b/80/23/0a/44.pdf.

Cotton, K. (2000). *Educating urban minority youth: Research on effective practices.* North West Regional Education Laboratory. (School Improvement Research Services Topical Synthesis #4). Retrieved March 30, 2007, from http:// www.nwrel.org.

Davis, J. (1994, April/May). A look at those who have decided to teach. *High School Journal 77*, 274–79.

Duarte, A. (2000). Wanted: 2 million teachers, especially minorities. *The Education Digest 66*(4), 19–23. Retrieved June 6, 2006, from http://vnweb.hwwilsonweb.com/ hww/results/results_single_ftPES.jhtml.

Eubanks, S. (1996). *The urban teacher challenge: A report on teacher recruitment and demand in selected Great City Schools.* Belmont, MA: Recruiting New Teachers, Inc.

Future Educators of Tomorrow [brochure]: Bloomington, IN: Phi Delta Kappa.

Gurskey, D. (1990). A plan that works. *Teacher, 1*(9): 46–54.

Haberman, M. (2005). *Star teachers: The ideology and best practice of effective teachers of diverse children and youth in poverty.* Houston, Texas: The Haberman Educational Foundation in association with Northeast Magic Consulting.

Haberman, M. (2002). *Achieving "High Quality" in the selection, preparation and retention of teachers.* Houston, Texas: The Haberman Educational Foundation, National Center for Alternative Teacher Certification Information. Retrieved March 10, 2009, from http://www.habermanfoundation .org/Articles/Default.asny?id=38.

Hallett, A., & Andrews, S. *Grow your own teachers: An Illinois initiative.* Retrieved March 24, 2008, from http://www .growyourownteachers.org/BeAnAdvocate/ GYO@20descriptionFeb%2008.pdf.

Harrington-Leucker, D. (Ed.). (1996). *The school personnel management system.* Alexandria, VA: National School Boards Association. Johnson, J., & Johnson, V. (1988).

Motivating minority students: Strategies that work. Springfield, IL: Charles C. Thomas.

Kearney, J. (2008). From camp to academy. A grow your own program model. *AASPA Perspective.* November 2007–January, 2008, pp. 16–17.

Kearney, J. (2007). *Minority Teacher Recruitment: If Not Now, When?* Overland Park, KS: American Association for School Personnel Administrators. Available at http://www.aaspa.org/assets/docs/Attachment_9_-_Minority_Recruitment_Publication.pdf.

Kearney, J. (2005). Factors affecting satisfaction and retention of African-American and European-American teachers in an urban school district: Implications for building and maintaining teachers employed in school districts across the nation. *Education and Urban Society Journal, 40*(5), 613–627.

Kearney, J. (2004, February-April). CAPE (Council attracting prospective educators): Ohio's strategy: Growing your own teachers. *AASPA Perspective,* p. 11.

Kearney, J. (1997). Factors affecting satisfaction and retention of African American and European American teachers in Columbus Public Schools (Doctoral dissertation, Ohio University, 1997). *Dissertation Abstracts International, 59*(4A),1026.

Melville, S., & Hall, S. (2001, May). Growing our own teachers extended learning and extra fun. *Classroom Leadership, 4*(8). Retrieved March 9, 2009, from http:/www.ascd.org/publications/classroom leadership/may2001/Growing Our Own Teachers.

* National Center for Educational Statistics, 1997

National Summit on Diversity in the Teaching Force. (2002, February 15). *Losing ground: A national summit on diversity in the teaching force.* [Proceedings document: Special report for AASPA members]. Washington, DC: Author.

Noeth, R., Engen, H., & Noeth, P. (1984, June). Making career decisions: A self-report of factors that helped high school students. *The Vocational Guidance Quarterly 32*(4), 242.

Northwest Regional Laboratory. (2001). *Educating minority youth.* Retrieved Jan. 1, 2009, from http://www.nwrel.org/scpd/sirs/5/topsyn4.html.

Northwest Regional Laboratory. (1997). *Closing the achievement gap requires multiple solutions.* Washington, DC: Author. Retrieved Nov. 8, 2009, from http://www.nwrel.org/cnorse/infoline/may97/article 5.htm.

*Ohio Department of Education, 1997.

Ohio Minority Recruitment Consortium. [Membership brochure.] See http://www.catalog.cpl.org/CLENIX?S=OHIO+MINORITY+RECRUITMENT+CONSORTIUM+1994.

Piercynski, M., Matranga, M., & Peltier, G. (1997, March/April). Legislative appropriations for minority teacher recruitment: Did it really matter? *Clearing House 77*(4), 205–206.

Ramirez, Eddy. (2007, Oct. 12). Grow your own teachers—Many of the best candidates already live in the neighborhood. *US News and World Report.* Available at http://www.usnews.com/articles/education/2007/10/12/grow-your-own-teachers.html.

Rasmussen, Karen. (January 1999). Preparing two million: How districts and states attract and retain teachers. *Education Update, (41)*1. Retrieved March 9, 2009, from http://www.ascd.org/publications/newsletters/education_update/jan99/vol41/num01/Preparing_Two_Million.aspx.

Recruiting New Teachers, Inc. (2004). *Silent crisis.* Retrieved July 5, 2004, from http://www.rnt.org/channels/clearinghouse/becometeacher/121_teachershort.htm.

Recruiting New Teachers, Inc., & Council of Great City Schools. (2000). *Urban Teacher Academy Project Tool Kit: A guide to developing high school teaching career academies.* Belmont, MA: Author.

Recruiting New Teachers, Inc. (1994). *Campaign Summary.* [Brochure]. Belmont, MA: Author.

Ribak-Rosenthal, N. (1994, January). Reasons individuals become school administrators, school counselors, and teachers. *School Counselor, 41,* 58–64.

Torres, J., Santos, J., Peck, N. L., & Cortes, L. (2004). *Minority teacher recruitment, development and retention.* Providence, RI: The Education Alliance at Brown University.

Villegas, A., & Lucas, T. (2002). *Educating culturally responsive teachers—A coherent approach*. Albany, NY: State University of New York.Urban Teacher Collaborative. (2000). *The urban teacher challenge. Teacher demand and supply in the Great City Schools*. [Report]. Belmont, MA: Author. Available at http://www.cgcs.org. and http://www.rnt.org.

Williams, M. (2007, March).*Human resource executives in the 21st century knowledge age: Partner or pariah*. Paper presented at the Ohio Association for School Personnel Administrators Conference.

Winston, M. (1997). *The role of recruitment in achieving goals related to diversity*. Retrieved March 30, 2007, from http://www.ala.org/ala/acrlbucket/nashville1997pap/winston.htm.